Walking the Path
with
Sai Baba

Walking the Path
with
Sai Baba

Howard Murphet

SAMUEL WEISER, INC.

York Beach, Maine

First published in 1993 by
Samuel Weiser, Inc.
Box 612
York Beach, Maine 03910-0612

99 98 97 96 95 94
10 9 8 7 6 5 4 3 2

Library of Congress Cataloging-in-Publication Data
Murphet, Howard.
        Walking the path with Sai Baba / by Howard Murphet.
            p.   cm.
        Previously published as : Sai Baba, invitation to glory,
1983.
        Includes bibliographical references.
        1. Sathya Sai Baba, 1926-   2. Hindus-India-
Biography.
    I. Title.
    BL1175.S385M885   1993
    294.5'092-dc20
    [B]   93-12651
                                                 CIP
ISBN 0-87728-781-3
MG

Typeset in 11 point Goudy

Printed in the United States of America

Contents

There shall move on earth, embodied and fair,
The living Truth of you.

—Sri Aurobindo
"A God's Labour"

Turn around Jerusalem;
His glory's on the wind.
He has come; He has come;
He has come again!

—from a song about Sai Baba
by Dennis Gersten

CHAPTER ONE

Sai Baba and You

"**Y**OU ARE GOD," I have heard Sai Baba say to people who question him about his own divinity. At such a statement, the questioner perhaps looks dumbfounded or disbelieving. Or, he may just appear wooden-faced, as if the statement—while acceptable academically—has little to do with reality. Yet this is the basic spiritual truth about our human identity that Baba is striving to inculcate.

The seeds of this truth were sown long ago in the Upanishadic wisdom of India, and have been fertilized through the centuries by many great world teachers, including Jesus, who said: "I am in my Father, and ye in me and I in you." (John 14:20).[1]

But we have tended to ignore, or gloss over, such remarks by our spiritual leaders. Knowing our own weaknesses and vices, it, no doubt, seems foolish, if not indeed blasphemous, to think of ourselves as being divine. And so we go on through the years and the generations engrossed, we are told, in our mortal dream, unaware that we are dreaming, or that there is a dreamer beyond the dream.

---

[1] All biblical references in this book come from *The Revised King James Version of the Holy Bible* (Oxford: Oxford University Press).

But if we accept, as a working hypothesis, that we human beings are in some non-understandable way parts of God—divine rays, perhaps, reflecting His image in many mirrors, or seeds dropped in the soil of earth from the Divine Tree—if this be so, how are we different from the ones we honor as messiahs, divine messengers, or avatars?

An American writer once remarked to Sai Baba, "If we are what you say, then we are all avatars—divine descents into matter." Some devotees, sitting in the room, were angry about this seemingly presumptuous observation. In one sense, however, it is true; in another, it is not. The basic difference is this—the avatar is aware of his descent and knows his divine identity. We, on the contrary, are not aware of our descent and are in complete ignorance about our identity.

That is the mortal error, or sense of separateness (the original sin) in which we are born. Swami explained this, pointing out gently that the only difference between him and us lies in the fact that he knows who he is, while we, who are basically the same, do not know it. Long ago the Buddha gave a similar explanation to his questioners. But he used the word *Buddha*, meaning Enlightened One, instead of the word *God*.

According to Hindu thought, there have been many descents in this avataric sense of an Enlightened One coming to earth. They are known as saints, prophets, Godmen, and so on. Each is aware, to some degree, of his or her identity with God. Hindu scriptures make it clear that these rays from the Divine vary in brightness, and therefore in their impact on the destiny of all beings here on earth.

But each has his or her important work to do in leading humanity toward the truth. The discarnate philosopher known as Seth[2] calls them "speakers," and supports the statements in the ancient books that they have come among us regularly throughout the legendary and forgotten aeons of the past.

In this galaxy of self-aware teachers, there appears from time to time a bright star who becomes known as a major avatar. He

---

[2] See *Seth Speaks* by Jane Roberts (Englewood Cliffs, NJ: Prentice-Hall, 1972).

is an evolutionary avatar who comes at the right moment to give humanity a spurt forward in its evolution. That moment coincides with a situation when the backward-pulling forces seem to be getting the upper hand, and humanity seems destined for utter destruction. The full avatar helps us through the great crisis, enabling us to learn through his suffering and begin a new dispensation. It seems that only the direct Hand of God can save the human ship from the rocks of destruction and steer it onto a new safe tack.

Some people—there are many of them—do not believe that an Avatar of God is necessary, or even possible. They believe that from His transcendent state on high—whatever that may mean—God can check the dark forces that are working against the divine plan, get things in balance again, and put us on the right course.

All things are possible to the omnipotent God, of course, and His ways and methods are beyond our understanding. Nevertheless, many who have delved deeply into the metaphysics of this great subject, from ancient time to now, believe that major, all-powerful avatars are a feature of the cosmic drama. Sai Baba puts it simply when he says, "You must dive into the pool to save a drowning man." And the poet-sage Aurobindo of Pondicherry wrote of the necessity of avatars:

> He who would bring the heavens here
> Must descend Himself into clay,
> And the burden of earthly nature bear,
> And tread the dolorous way.[3]

Putting such difficult metaphysical concepts aside, our experience shows that from time to time there does appear on earth one who seems more than human—one whose superhuman powers and lofty nature are clearly demonstrated to all who spend time with him. Such great ones have a tremendous im-

---

[3] Sri Aurobindo, from a poem titled "A God's Labour" in *The Hidden Manner* (Pondicherry, India: Sri Aurobindo Press, n.d.).

pact on the people of their times, being greatly loved by some and greatly hated by others. And so, of course, they become controversial figures. Jesus Christ was one such; Sai Baba is another.

But the waters of two thousand years have flowed under the bridge of time since God's Messiah was nailed to a cross. It is high time that we came to a better understanding of God and nature and human beings.

We can begin by ceasing to regard the "laws of nature" as something fixed, irrevocable and all-inclusive. We should see them as what they are—our attempt to give a systematic coherent explanation of the natural phenomena we encounter. But because we are still probing and have not yet probed to the depths of nature, our laws cannot be more than partial explanations. As we go deeper into subatomic physics, and outward into the galaxies of the cosmos, new explanations are needed and new laws of nature—often cancelling out the old ones—are formulated. Revisions, amendments, sometimes complete reversals of the explanations have been in process since the beginnings of science, and will continue to be so until the deepest secrets of nature are laid bare. And within the powers of the present level of our Earth consciousness, that will be never.

Probing into the seemingly endless divisibility of the atom is taking the human mind beyond itself—into ideas and concepts that are no longer rational. Even the basic axioms of logical thinking have to be abandoned. Possible explanations appear to demand the paradoxical logic of mystical insights. So the new, more embracing laws of nature that must be formulated will seem to contradict some of the old laws—as miracles seem to.

St. Augustine understood what many people do not understand even today. He wrote: "Miracles do not happen in contradiction to nature, but only in contradiction to man's current laws of nature."[4]

Whether or not you accept the miracles of olden times—those of Krishna, Buddha, Christ—the fact remains that the

---

[4] F. C. Happold, *Mysticism* (New York: Viking Penguin, 1963).

miracles of Sai Baba have been taking place, for living people to see, during some five decades now. They have been witnessed, experienced, attested by thousands of intelligent, trustworthy men and women of many countries.

Incidentally, it was through experiencing the Sai miracles, and proving to myself their undeniable authenticity, that I came to believe in the miracles of the old days, and looked with new eyes at that wonderful, ever-changing, never-stable appearance we call nature. Then I understood that the Age of Miracles is not something that has passed. It is now; it always was; it ever will be.

It may help us today to understand and accept the reality of the miraculous if we see it in relationship to ourselves. For there is a very real relationship. When we witness and experience the miraculous powers, wisdom, and pure love of Sai Baba, we may feel that a great gulf lies between him and us. Indeed, there is a gulf, and its name is "ignorance." Baba can go on telling us, over and over again, that we are one with him, the same as him, part of the highest Divinity, but we still cannot cross the Gulf of Ignorance. If we could find the craft to sail across those broad waters, and see the light dawn on the far shore of the gulf, we would then know great things and be forever free.

The greatest thing we would know for certain—not by inference, not by being told, but by direct, intuitive knowing—would be that (as Swami reiterates) we are, indeed, one with God, with all life, with the whole universe. Two important things would result from that sure knowledge. One, we would be set free from our serfdom to the desires and cravings of the senses; and two, we would be flooded with that selfless love that is a permanent attribute of Divinity. Being thus above and beyond the self-centered, carnal calls of nature, we would find ourselves with power over nature. Power which, from the ordinary human point of view, appears to be miraculous.

The twin of this divine power, born at the same time of the same mother, is, as we said, divine love. This will prevent us from using the newly acquired power in any way that is destructive and detrimental to other people.

It will be helpful to our understanding to note, however, that there are degrees of extraordinary powers—some of them manifesting before the full light of wisdom dawns on the far side of the Gulf of Ignorance.

Even when at death we cast off the limiting fetters of the body, and find ourselves on one of the subtle intermediate planes, we may be surprised to discover that we have certain "miraculous" powers. This has been taught in some of the ancient writings on the after-death state. For example, *The Tibetan Book of the Dead* expresses it this way:

> Thou art actually endowed with the power of miraculous action (power to change one's shape, size and number, to appear as one or many, to appear or disappear at will). . . . thou canst instantaneously arrive in whatever place thou wishest; thou hast the power of reaching there within the time which a man taketh to bend, or to stretch forth his hand. . . . None is there [of such powers] which thou mayst desire which thou canst not exhibit.[5]

Different avenues of modern psychic research support the teachings of the ancient texts, and confirm that these powers and others, such as telepathy and clairvoyance, are normal to the disembodied soul on certain after-death planes.

Such psychic faculties are inherent within us while we are still imprisoned in the flesh, and occasionally reveal their presence as clairvoyance, telepathy, precognition, or in some other way. With most people, this is rather like a door opening and closing again, quickly, but with a few individuals one or more of the psychic faculties may remain active, in a partly manifested state, for years or even for a lifetime. These are the clairvoyants, the fortune-tellers, and so on.

---

[5] *The Tibetan Book of the Dead* (Oxford: Oxford University Press, 1960), p. 159.

But such powers are partial, faulty, and incomplete when compared with our inherent divine powers. They are a kind of halfway house between the human and divine natures. Yet they do illustrate the point that we hold within ourselves the seeds of divine attributes.

Patanjali, and other great sages expounding the yoga philosophy, teach that through right practice, techniques of self-control, and self-discipline many of our inherent "miraculous" powers will fructify, and come under the control of our will, while we are still in the physical body. An essential part of yoga training is to develop the moral character of the pupil so that he or she will not use the manifesting yogic powers in a wrong way. Furthermore, the aim and purpose of this intense yoga of will power, known as Raja Yoga, is to reach union with God. The powers that manifest along the route are never the aim. If the pupil treats them as such, he or she has failed.

When we understand this deep psychology—our latent powers and divine goal—which Bhagavan Sai Baba is teaching, we will not feel that there is anything weird, far-out, or mind boggling in the flow of Sai miracles. We will see that Swami is demonstrating to us what God is and, therefore, what we are. He is showing us what we are potentially, and what we will become actually when we throw off the bonds of time and space, and follow along his holy way.

We can, if we will, see our true Selves reflected in him; see that he is, in fact, the real Self of each of us. Swami, like all great Teachers, is fond of giving parables and allegories to reveal great truths at different levels to different levels of understanding. All people gain something this way. I, myself, think of his miracles as parables in action as they tell us more dramatically than parables what we are, and what we will become.

In words he says: "Within you is the mighty ocean of nectar divine." From that ocean within will come the joy, love, and creativity that he is forever demonstrating. By looking more closely at the Sai parables, given both in action and in words, we may learn the sooner to turn our footsteps from the dolorous way of earth to the Way of Divine Delight.

CHAPTER TWO

Psychic
and Divine Healing

"**B**EHOLD THOU ART made whole: sin no more" (John 8:11), said Jesus to a man he had just healed. This cryptic remark holds the clue to the deepest levels in the art of healing. When the body is ill, the cause lies beyond the body. Medical research is finding that even the common cold has its origin in the mind. Viruses are concerned, yes, but it is a certain negative state of mind that permits a virus to enter and become active so that an unbalanced, dis-eased condition results. Medical opinion is now allowing more and more complaints to be classed as psychosomatic diseases. But it certainly would not agree that all disease has its origin in mental and emotional conditions. Yet in the end this may prove to be so.

The majority of diseases respond to treatment by modern medical science. But there are many that do not, and then what, if any, is the cure? There are, of course, other therapies that can be tried, and in practice many have proved successful where orthodox medicine has failed. Yet the medical profession is reluctant to admit this, and strives to keep the lucrative business of healing exclusively to itself.

There are, however, notable exceptions to this attitude among individual medical men. Some are joining in with holistic healing groups that aim to treat the whole person—body, mind, and soul. Others have joined in research into therapies that the profession in general treats with deep suspicion.

One of these is psychic healing. This method of treatment has been going on in many parts of the world for a very long time. But during recent decades it has become concentrated in two areas—the Philippines and Brazil. Researchers have visited both places, but teams of research workers, including medical people and scientists, have gone mainly to the Philippines. The findings have given rise to a good deal of publicity, but, judging by serious writings coming from members of the research teams themselves,[1] most of the publicity has been unbalanced, and has given the wrong impression.

It has highlighted the fakes, leading to the impression that all the Philippine phenomena are sham. Yet research workers discovered, along with some fakery, a good deal of genuine phenomena, and some successful healing. Research also revealed some interesting facts about the methods and motivations of the healers, and the forces that work through them.

Having had personal contact with patients returning from the Philippines (some cured, some helped, and some not), my wife and I decided to take a look at the scene ourselves. By on-the-spot observation we would be in a better position to understand what the situation really was. The questions to be answered were: was it all a hoax, or were some healers genuine, and successful in their psychic efforts? What was the power behind them? Would people given up by Western medical science have any chance of a cure in the Philippines?

We were planning a visit to the great Divine Healer in India, so decided to make a stopover in the Philippines, and try to gather some firsthand experience and information about the psychic healing there. Thus it was, that, armed with a list of healers' names, and vague indications of their possible where-

---

[1] *Healers and the Healing Process*, edited by George W. Meek (Wheaton, IL: Theosophical Publishing House, 1977).

abouts, we landed in Manila. We did not have time to study the whole scene, but hoped to be able to observe a few healers at work. In this way we might be able to form a conclusion, at least satisfactory to ourselves, and perhaps of interest to others.

At the "surgery" of the first healer we visited, we found ourselves waiting with a crowd of about twenty patients in a kind of chapel. It was rather a dingy place, this chapel, in the gray light of early morning. Also there was the indescribable musty atmosphere that one finds in some spiritist centers. I have long tried to analyze the cause of this typical psychic atmosphere, and can only think that it is brought about by the presence of unprogressed, earth-clinging spirits. Anyway, the atmosphere labeled the healing center as spiritist. This did not condemn it, in our view, but merely suggested its nature.

When the healer, an obliging fellow, knew that we were there to observe, he invited us into his operating room. For one of his patients whose skin he wished to open, he took my index finger, and, holding it in his hand about eighteen inches from the bare skin, he made a quick downward movement in the air as if my finger was a knife. A scratch some inches long appeared on the skin below where this cutting gesture was made.

I had heard of this psycho-kinetic phenomenon, practiced by some of the healers, and was pleased to witness it. But I was disappointed that the opening made was no more than a deep scratch. However, it seemed to be all the healer needed. He drew blood from the opening, and began taking what seemed to be short strings of fibrous material from the blood and showing them to the patient.

For another patient, a Westerner, stretched out on the operating table, the psychic surgeon made no skin opening, but began taking what looked like small pieces of flesh from near the man's genital organs. His finger tips seemed to feel along the surface of the skin, without entering, yet the pieces of "flesh" came into them. He must have taken six or seven pieces, and tossed them into a bowl of water before he allowed the patient to leave the table and the room.

Following the man out into the chapel, I learned from him that he had been suffering from a swollen prostate gland, and that this was his third session on the operating table. Never had he felt any pain or ill effects from these operations in which the healer claimed to be taking flesh from his swollen prostate. This was his final treatment, and the healer assured him that his prostate was now back to normal size. He, himself, seemed optimistic about it, but not entirely confident, as the healer would not let him take away the pieces of matter allegedly from his prostate.

But if not from there, as claimed, where were the pieces from? They had not been in the healer's fingers when he began the operation. We (that is, a friend, my wife who is a trained nurse, and I) had watched very closely and could detect no sleight-of-hand. It certainly looked as if the pieces of flesh-like matter had been apported to the surgeon's fingers, either from inside the body or from some distance outside it. But if it was in fact the patient's own flesh, why wouldn't the healer let him take it away for analysis? And was the man really cured?

Finding that the patient was Australian, I took his address, hoping to be able to check sometime later if this had proved a genuine cure or not. Two years afterward I met him in Australia and found that he still had a swollen prostate gland. There had been no apparent improvement from the psychic surgery.

A failure to effect a cure is not, of course, something for which we should condemn a healer. Even our best doctors have their failures, and some of them will, at times, indulge in a little fakery if it will help psychologically toward a cure.

With this particular healer we did not detect any trickery. But it is of interest that later on in Hong Kong we met a lady who had worked with the healer for a time. She said that his opening of the skin from a distance was normally genuine, but that at times when his psychic power was running low, he would resort to trickery. He would have a piece of razor blade hidden in cotton wool, make a scratch with this as he swabbed the skin, then immediately perform the finger-pointing act. The scratch, a slight one, would not show plainly until the cutting finger gesture was carried out. Then it would appear as if produced by the mysterious psychic power.

A study of the situation indicates that the main cause of fakery among the healers is greed. Many years ago, when psychic healing was practiced in the simple villages, the healers received only modest material rewards. They had gone through psychic and mediumistic training, but were not always full-time healers. They labored in the fields with the other villagers and healed the sick when required. Any payment they received made them no richer than the other peasant folk with whom they lived. They had a healing gift, and their main motivation was the desire to heal.

But then came the hordes from the West, looking for wonder cures, and ready to pay handsomely for such services. Some healers moved into the cities and tourist centers to exploit the situation. Dreams of wealth lured them to accept all comers. The daily stream of foreign patients grew larger, demanding the expenditure of more and more psychic power.

Psychic power has its limits and when it runs low, what then? Fake it. If the patient believes it is genuine, it will have the required effect in raising belief, the placebo effect, an important ingredient in all healing. Even if there was no immediate cure, the relatively wealthy patients from the West were likely to make substantial donations to the wonder-workers, trusting that the cure would result, as the healer assured them, with the passage of time.

Thousands have made such donations, and some healers are now wealthy property owners. But by gaining materially through over-working their powers, by replacing compassionate desire to heal with selfish desire for wealth, their psychic power has weakened. So, with some of them for most of the time, and with most of them for some of the time, tricks of conjury play a part in their psychic operations.

One of the healers in whose work the visiting researchers from abroad had detected no trickery was Josephine Sisson. She was reported to have brought about some remarkable cures, and she had a reputation for complete honesty. It is interesting that she still lives and works in the village of her birth.

To visit her we came down from the highlands of Baguio and got a room in a little hotel just outside the town of Urdaneta. It is a hot spot, but pleasant with great green plains of rice stretching to the skyline. Strangely, most of the psychic healers were born in villages of this lush rice bowl, but the majority of them had moved away.

From the hotel we hired a car to take us to Josephine's village of Baronggabong. The proprietor sent along one of his waitresses to act as guide and interpreter. After a few miles on the main road to Manila we turned onto a dirt road riddled with potholes. About three miles of low gear crawling along this brought us to the little village of Baronggabong. All the houses were thatched, had flimsy frame walls, and ducks, fowl, pigs, and other livestock wandering freely around them.

The driver did not need the waitress to guide him into New Pig-pen Road where he stopped in front of a house that already had several other cars parked in front. This was Josephine's surgery.

It had the same simple farmyard atmosphere as the other houses, but in front of it stood a neat little chapel. Into this we went. Inside, a man, who proved to be Josephine's uncle, was reading the Bible in English from the platform. After the reading he preached, mainly on the theme of the power of prayer in healing. There were about twenty people present, among them a group of Americans. The chapel was clean and bright.

At the end of the service two women entered and sat on the platform. I knew intuitively which of the two was Josephine: she had a soft, gentle face with large, dark, expressive eyes.

The chapel was also the surgery. People came up onto the platform in the order in which they were sitting in the pews. From where we sat we could see Josephine treating them. But we wanted to have a closer look than was possible in this way, so we decided to be patients ourselves.

When our turn came, we went up onto the platform. Iris told the healer about some kidney weakness she had had for a long time. Josephine took a piece of paper and with a pencil absently wrote some strange characters on it. I had read previously that when she could not get a satisfactory diagnosis by clairvoyance or clairaudience, she used automatic writing. So the piece of paper evidently contained the diagnosis.

She put Iris on the operating table, drew curtains across to hide us from the people in the pews and asked Iris to bare her abdomen down to the hips. As the husband, I was permitted to remain. I stood right by Josephine's hands as she worked.

She began kneading my wife's lower abdomen with both hands, the fingers going inside the skin. A lake of blood spread over the abdomen. This was mopped away from time to time by the other woman who was evidently Josephine's assistant. With my eyes not more than eighteen inches from the healer's hands I could clearly see the fingers going into the body beyond the first joint and the blood oozing out around them. Yet, oddly, it seemed a little lighter in color, and thinner in consistency, than normal blood appears to be. The reason for this I do not know.

Presently Josephine took out a thin piece of corroded metal about an inch in length. She showed it to me with an expression of surprise.

"Where is it from?" I asked.

"I don't know. It just came into my fingers."

She gave it to me and continued to probe. Soon she brought out another piece of metal, the same type but a little shorter. "They would not do your kidneys any good," she told Iris, handing me the second piece also. The patient was quite conscious, seeing all, but, as she told me later, feeling nothing whatever.

Josephine continued to probe for a while, dipping her fingers every now and then into a bowl of water on the table. Sometimes she would extract a piece of fibrous matter from the blood, examine it, and throw it into a receptacle, into which the blood-soaked cotton wool also went. When the operation was over, the skin closed automatically leaving no mark.

I was next for the operating table. I decided to tell the healer about the poor hearing in my right ear. Several years earlier a specialist in Australia had said that the cause was probably a small occlusion in a blood vessel connected with the ear. "There is no cure, but you'll get used to it," he had declared.

While I was on the operating table my wife watched Josephine take what appeared to be a dark-colored cyst from below the skin near the right ear. I saw nothing and felt nothing.

"Now you'll be all right," Josephine assured me.

"But my hearing is no better."

"It will gradually get better as time goes on."

If there had been a blockage of blood, deadening a nerve, it was reasonable to assume that the nerve would take time to return to normal, following the removal of the blockage. So I accepted her statement and felt hopeful.

At the end of our session with Josephine the name of Sai Baba was mentioned in conversation. Josephine's reaction to the name was remarkable. Her eyes lit up; her serene face became radiant, animated.

"Sai Baba!" she echoed. "He sometimes helps me. His presence . . . his vibration is so strong, so powerful! Oh! I can't express it. . . ." She seemed at a loss for words.

When we told her that we were on our way to see Sai Baba, she said, "Please give him my love." We had the impression that, whatever her ability as a healer, Josephine was honest, genuine, and had a true spiritual quality.

We felt quite uplifted as we went out through the little chapel, and were pleased that our names would be there in the long list of those whom Josephine and her religious uncle pray for daily "until they were cured," as he assured us.

About the two pieces of corroded metal, we wondered and thought a good deal. Ben Felix, an old theosophist and retired engineer from Manila, told us it was the type of magnetic metal that would travel about inside the body. Then Iris began to think they might be connected with a major bone operation for a spine graft she had undergone in England some thirty years earlier. Was it possible that these two pieces—one with a small hook at the end—were the remains of a broken surgical clip left in her body by mistake? They looked like it, she said. Later we showed the pieces to a medical man who had performed many operations on wounded soldiers in England during the Second World War. He confirmed that they were just like the surgical clips used in bone operations at that period. "Very probably they are from a clip left in your body," he told Iris, after hearing about her orthodox operation in England and the strange unorthodox one performed in the Philippines.

There is certainly some psychic, non-physical power behind the work of the Philippine surgeons and healers. They, themselves, seem to have no doubt that this is a spiritist power. The healers know nothing about anatomy or physiology and practice none of the rules of medical hygiene. But they have had training as spiritist mediums.

When treating a patient, the healers are in a type of light trance sometimes called a "mystical union." They are themselves conscious, but to varying degrees are possessed or over-shadowed by some other conscious power that manipulates their hands—to open the body for surgical operations, or to bring a healing force into the body.

The healers have a background of Roman Catholicism, but belong to the Christian Spiritist Union of the Philippines (Union Espiritista Cristiana de las Filipinas), which the Roman Church does not accept. Nevertheless many of the healers seem to be fervently religious people, imbued with a simple faith. Some of them say it is the Holy Spirit or God working through them. Others name a Christian saint who is their "protector." Still others are vague on the matter, and do not identify the healing power that comes through their minds and hands.

Though their healing is essentially mediumistic, that is, they are instruments through which a power greater than their normal selves works, they are sometimes called "faith healers." Perhaps faith in the Divine Power, shared by both healer and patient, does play a part in any genuine cures that take place.

In fact, it is said that the automatic opening of the body and the sight of blood are really for the purpose of enhancing faith in the minds of the sophisticated patients from cities and Western lands. Back in their villages, before they became world famous, the healers worked mainly by the "laying on" of hands in the manner of faith healers. Their unsophisticated patients had enough faith in the power of the spirits working through the healers to bring about the necessary cures.

Though he does sometimes practice open-body psychic surgery, a healer who still uses the laying on of hands to a large degree is Vergillio Guttierez, who has a healing center in Manila. We found him a humble, unpretentious, likeable man, able to give remarkable diagnoses simply by using his hands to feel vibrations in different parts of the body.

The slightest disharmony in any organ of the body revealed itself to him in this way, and he named, for my wife and me, the different diseases we had suffered since childhood, as well as any current weaknesses. He proved to be a more accurate and thorough diagnostician than any medical expert I had ever met—with the possible exception of the Steiner healer, Dr. Siegfried Knauer.

But we were not able to test his healing ability as we were scheduled to leave the Philippines the day after we met him. When we told him that we were on our way to India, he said:

"Ah! You must see Sai Baba when you are there."

"That is the purpose of our journey."

"Oh, well, tell him that the 'fake healer' is all right," he said, smiling. We learned that he had, himself, been to see Swami and been labeled the "fake healer." He was obviously not offended by this, understanding that it was only Baba's mischievous play on the words "faith healer."

After our visit to Guttierez, we went for lunch to our favorite vegetarian restaurant, and there talked to a young couple we had seen that morning sitting with the patients in the Guttierez chapel. They proved to be from Melbourne, Australia.

The husband, who was riddled with cancer, had been given up by the doctors, but was hoping for a miracle cure in the Philippines. Strangely, it was through a friend of ours, Dr. Ian Gawler, that the couple were making this last desperate bid. They had, they said, heard about Dr. Gawler's case through the media in Australia, and contacted him. He had suggested that they try Vergillio Guttierez.

They had been visiting Guttierez for some weeks when we met them and the husband said he was feeling some changes within his body that could be significant. He did not, however, seem very optimistic about a cure.

We felt a tremendous hope that this fellow countryman of ours would somewhere, sometime, find a cure, for the sake of his young wife and children.[2]

This brings us to the case of our remarkable friend, the veterinary surgeon, Ian Gawler. Prolonged treatment for bone cancer by orthodox medical methods had resulted in the amputation of one of Ian's legs, but had brought no improvement to his condition. As a last desperate measure, he decided to try the psychic healers in the Philippines.

During two visits covering several months, Ian consulted some fifteen different psychic healers. About six of them, including Vergillio Guttierez, had, he said, proved "consistently useful."

In fact, after the months of treatment in the Philippines, Ian was told that his cancer was cured, but that he should go to Sai Baba in India for the inner mental cure that would ensure the disease did not return.

Dr. Gawler said that he had by nature always been a sceptic, and that his scientific training had made him more so. Now, even though the symptoms were no longer there, he felt that he might not really be cured; it may be only a "recession."

Both he and his wife, Gayle, decided that, just in case it might help, they should make the trip to India and try to see Sai Baba. The most important thing in their lives was for Ian to return to permanent good health.

---

[2] We learned some two years later that the young man had died in Melbourne.

When they arrived in India, they found that Swami was visiting Ootacamund (Ooty) in the Nilgiri Hills, where he has a school for young children. They went there and waited with the crowd in the garden outside his house. When Baba came out to give *darshan*, he invited Ian and Gayle inside, and, as they crossed the threshold of the interview room, he looked at Ian and said, "You are already healed!"

This assurance from the Divine Healer, himself, was just what Ian needed to remove his lingering doubts and establish his faith. Then Swami produced *vibhuti* for him, and showered love on both of them.

They remained near Lord Sai for as long as possible, basking in his aura of divine love and grace, confident that Ian was getting that inner deep cure that would remove the roots of the terrible disease and prevent any recurrence. After a brief and necessary trip back to Australia, they returned to the feet of Sai and remained for a longer period, "just to enjoy more of his love and grace," they said.

By determination and persistence, Ian Gawler had, he believed, achieved a cure through the psychic healers in the Philippines. Sai Baba had confirmed this when he announced, "You are already healed." Then, the inner workings of Baba's divine alchemy would, they both felt confident, keep the killer disease permanently at bay. It was a wonderful thought, bright with hope for the future.

That was several years ago and time has confirmed their hope. Dr. Gawler has built up his professional practice again in Australia. The couple now have two children (born since the cure), and are living normal happy lives—thanks to psychic and divine healing, plus that very essential, positive faith, and the will for life and health.

Researchers state that there is not sufficient statistical evidence to enable them to say what proportion of actual cures take place, but some estimate that there is a small proportion of immediate cures, and a substantial proportion of cures that take place over a period of time (weeks or months), as in the case of

Ian Gawler. A fair percentage of patients, it seems, obtains some relief from their conditions, though not a complete cure. My wife, for example, feels that the long-standing weakness in her kidneys has improved since Josephine Sisson removed the broken clip left behind by careless surgery. I, myself, belong to what research suggests is the largest category: those who obtain no benefit at all. The hearing in my right ear has not improved as Josephine assured me it would. Perhaps my name is still on the paper prayer flags flying at her chapel, and who knows? Prayer, plus faith, plus time, may eventually wear away whatever bad karma is giving me this slight disability.

The laborer is worthy of his hire, as the Bible says. But if the laborer thinks of nothing but his material rewards, he will not be of much use in the vineyard of psychic healing. Apart from his power weakening, he may attract the wrong kind of forces and become a negative influence, doing more harm than good to his patients. This is a situation about which people should be watchful and discerning.

But we know from personal experience that there are at least some healers who do not seem to be concerned about material rewards. If you wish to make a donation to Josephine, for instance, you put the money in a drawer and she, herself, pays no attention to what you are doing in this regard. Guttierez is another who gave us the impression that he was not at all concerned with what, if anything, a patient puts in the donation box. There are others, however, who know well enough how to bring psychological pressure to bear to make sure the patient hands them a big donation. With them you feel it is business first and all the way.

On the whole, our personal observations confirmed the conclusions of the research workers. It is a very mixed scene in the Philippines—a mixture of failure and success, of fakery and real psychic power, of commercialization and a genuine, sympathetic desire to heal the sick. Psychic spiritist "surgery" has a place in the broad spectrum of healing arts, but it cannot be classed with the divine healing of an enlightened Master.

It is not always best for our spiritual welfare that we be relieved of our disabilities at a particular point in time. The compassionate enlightened Master knows just when a cure can and should be effected, and when the deep roots of a disease should be plucked out swiftly, or drawn out gently and slowly.

The Parachutist

When I first saw him standing there, in Swami's anteroom at Brindavan, Whitefield, I would never have guessed that this man had been the champion parachute jumper of the Indian Air Force. So gentle he seemed, and humble, with an intense spiritual fire burning in his dark eyes

Humble Sri A. Chakravati was, and is, spiritual in an honest, unpretentious way; his ancestors had for generations been hereditary gurus in a village in East Bengal where he was born. But when, as the eldest son, he was asked to take the position at his father's death, he refused, considering himself unworthy of such a high, spiritually responsible position.

He was 17 at the time, and began working on a newspaper in Calcutta while continuing post-graduate studies at the university there. He obtained his Master of Arts degree before the Second World War broke out, and he joined the Indian Air Force. Through a special examination he was able to gain a commission as pilot officer. He seems to have had the qualities that led to swift promotion to the rank of Squadron Leader, and the courage that made him the champion parachutist of the Air Force.

By the end of the war he was in command of India's parachute jumping school. Senior Royal Air Force officers and other important officials came out from Britain to visit his school, and he, himself, was sent to the United Kingdom on several occasions. There, he was treated as a VIP.

"I became too proud," he said. I found that hard to believe. But he must have made some errors, and doubtless his rapid promotion and renown had built up a bank of envious enemies. Whatever the cause, he found himself suddenly transferred to a remote Air Force station in Jammu.

No married quarters were provided, and the only house he could find had a leaky roof and quite inadequate heating facilities for the cold months that were upon them. Chakravati worried about the discomforts as his wife was pregnant with their first child. The child was still-born. Furthermore, due to medical mistakes, he thinks, his wife contracted a disease of the uterus. Being a contagious condition, it was passed on to the husband.

All the doctors they were able to consult told the couple that it was a rare disease and quite incurable. Moreover, it would prevent them ever having children.

This was a very sad and gloomy situation. With no hope of a family, his career prospects clouded, condemned to suffer an unpleasant disease for life, the couple began reading for solace a book on the great Indian saints. When they came to the life of Sai Baba of Shirdi, a gleam of light illumined their hearts. Over and over again they read the story aloud to each other. It brought them warmth and comfort as they sat huddled in their chilly house under the leaky roof.

Then they began to pray: "Sai Baba, if you are still somewhere on Earth, let us come to you." They knew nothing of his reincarnation as Satya Sai, but obviously they had hopes that he might be here in some way, somewhere.

Soon afterward Squadron Leader A. Chakravati was transferred to Jallahalli, near Bangalore. Before long he met and became friendly with another Bengali. This was Dr. D. K. Banerjee, who was then Professor of Organic Chemistry at the All India Institute of Science in Bangalore.

It was someone else, however, who told Chakravati the great news that there was a saint-yogi called Satya Sai Baba who had an ashram at Puttaparti, just over a hundred miles north of Bangalore. The Squadron Leader's heart leapt at the name. This, he felt, must be the Sai Baba to whom he had prayed so often, so fervently.

He told his friend Banerjee about it. "Let us go together and see him; you have a car," he urged the scientist.

Banerjee demurred. "I've heard various things about him. No, I'm not keen to go."

But Chakravati was determined to go, and determined that his friend should go, too. He repeated the request persistently over the next few weeks until, finally, Banerjee gave way and agreed.

All this was taking place toward the end of 1961, before Swami had a residence at Whitefield near Bangalore. It was actually on November 18, 1961, that the two friends, with another scientist from the Institute, set off along the bumpy road that wound through the barren hills to a remote village ignored by all the signposts, but one that mentioned Puttaparti apologetically in rustic lettering.

At the gates of the ashram a boy ran out and offered them a key, with the surprising words, "Baba has allotted room No. 9 to you and your party, Dr. Banerjee."

As they had sent no word of their coming, Chakravati was amazed and impressed. Dr. Banerjee was not.

They put their bags in No. 9, and made their way to the front of the Mandir, then a much smaller building than at present. The sun had set and darkness was falling. Only one bare electric globe burned before the building where about a hundred people were waiting for darshan. The three new arrivals waited, too.

Suddenly Baba was there, standing on the balcony. "I felt he was someone I had lost long ago and now found again," Chakravati said. "Tears began to pour down my cheeks; I was glad we were in the darkness under the trees."

Soon afterward Baba sent someone to call them in for an interview. As they entered the room, Swami did a strange thing. He gave Dr. Banerjee a hug and said enigmatically, "So, you have come at last. . . ." (Did this mean that Banerjee had been a devotee in a former life?) Then Swami gave the doctor another blessing by producing a locket from the air and handing it to him.

After talking for about forty-five minutes on spiritual sub-jects to the three of them, Baba turned to Chakravati and made him cup his hands together to form a bowl. Above the bowl Swami held his own down-turned palm, waving it gently back and forth. Vibhuti poured from the divine palm in a constant stream until it filled Chakravati's cupped hands to the brim.

"Eat it!" Baba said. It was a tall order, but the Squadron Leader obeyed.

On the following day the party was called for another inter-view during which Swami materialized things for Banerjee and the other scientist. Then again he instructed Chakravati to cup his hands together as before. Again Baba waved his palm above them until they brimmed with vibhuti. Once more the Air Force officer was ordered to eat the holy ash, and consumed the large quantity to the last grain. "It had a delicate flavor," he said.

On the morning after their return to Bangalore, Chakravati found, to his utter amazement and inexpressible joy, that he was free of his "incurable" disease. Even more astounding was the fact that his wife was cured, too. The two massive doses of vibhuti had wrought a double cure.

About a month later Chakravati and Dr. Banerjee took their wives to Puttaparti. During an interview Swami asked Mrs. Chakravati, "Have you no children?" The question was, she felt, rhetorical, as he obviously knew the answer.

"This year," Swami told her, "you will have a son." Cha-kravati could not help laughing aloud at this. "Why do you laugh?" asked Baba.

"All the four doctors who have examined my wife said that she cannot have any children, Swami. Now you say she will have a son!"

Baba crossed the index fingers of his two hands, and, look-ing into Chakravati's eyes, said, "When Swami makes a sankalpa, it becomes siddha."—meaning, Swami's will is always accomplished.

At that moment the descendant of a long line of spiritual leaders knew for certain that he was in the presence of an Avatar of God.

Swami added, "In November this year you will get a son; a very good soul is coming to you. I shall personally visit your home to name the boy."

Before the interview was over, Baba created a locket for Mrs. Chakravati; it bore the image of Lord Rama. She was surprised and rather disappointed at this as she had always worshiped the form of Lord Krishna. In fact, during the ensuing weeks she complained several times to her husband about getting the image of Rama instead of Krishna.

But Chakravati was more interested in the wonderful prophecy about a son. He told his medical friend at the Military Hospital about it. The doctor was amused, and remarked, "If saints and sadhus can give barren people children, medical science is superfluous."

During June of that year, 1962, Mrs. Chakravati thought she was pregnant and the Squadron Leader asked his sceptical doctor friend to come and examine her. He came one Sunday, bringing a staff nurse from the hospital with him. After a thorough examination, the doctor gave the couple his verdict: "Sorry, there's no child. It's all gas."

Their hopes were dashed. How could a son be born in November, only five months away, if she was not pregnant now?

One day, soon after the doctor's announcement, the Chakravati couple were invited to the home of Dr. Banerjee, where Swami was paying a visit. They did not have to tell the omniscient Lord what the military doctor had said. He knew already and repeated it to them as they sat at his feet. "But," he added, "don't worry, you will have a son. He will be born on November 23rd this year." Now they believed again, and were doubly thrilled because the 23rd was Swami's own birthday.

The Avatar gave a further example of the omniscience to which they were becoming accustomed when he said to Mrs. Chakravati, "You have been complaining about the Rama locket Swami gave you." He waved his hand and took another locket from the air. Handing this to her he said, "Here, take your Krishna!" The locket had an image of Krishna on one side and Shirdi Sai Baba on the other.

That night Mrs. Chakravati definitely felt the stirrings of life in her womb and knew for certain that a child was there. Even the doubting doctor had to admit she was pregnant when next he was called to examine her. And he agreed to have her admitted to the Military Hospital before the predicted date of birth.

Yet, when the morning of the 23rd dawned, the doctors and hospital nurses were concerned that the birth would not take place for some days. The expectant mother felt sad about this as she dearly wanted her child to be born on Swami's birthday, as he had foretold.

When the night nurse took over in the evening, she asked her patient why she was looking so downcast instead of happy at the forthcoming event.

"Oh, a great saint told me I would have a son on this day. But I'm sorry to say the doctors and nurses tell me it will not be born for some days yet."

"Who was the saint?"

"Sai Baba."

"Well, if Sai Baba said your child will be born today, it certainly will be! Now, come along to the labor ward."

As they went, Mrs. Chakravati asked, "Are you, then, a follower of Sai Baba?"

"No, I'm a Christian. But I've heard about him and I know he's a great prophet. What he says will be, will be!"

The nurse made her patient walk up and down in the labor ward, while she, herself, began arranging all that was necessary for the delivery of the baby. Very late that night, without any pain, Mrs. Chakravati gave birth to a son.

After the event, the doctor who had laughed at the prophecy became a devotee of Sai Baba. In due course the Lord came to their home and named the boy Krishnakishora, which means "little Krishna." The parents remembered the drama of the lockets, the mother's yearning toward Krishna and Swami's words: "A good soul is coming to you." What strange mysteries lie behind the door of human birth? How can we know, knowing only a child is born?

As the years passed, many events showed that the Lord, who had brought them health and happiness, was looking after the welfare of parents and child, and that distance was no barrier to this.

Once, for instance, when they were living back in the north of India, Krishnakishora fell ill and the doctors diagnosed asthma.

"After giving us this child, Swami, how can you let him get asthma, an incurable disease!" the mother mentally reproached Baba, a thousand miles away in Puttaparti.

The Squadron Leader wrote to Dr. Banerjee, begging him to ask Swami for directions. Swami's reply was: "The mother is complaining to me about letting the boy get asthma. She should blame herself for letting the *ayah* (nurse) take him out in the cold and wet. But it's not asthma, only bronchitis. He will soon be better."

The doctors, examining the child again, found only bronchitis, and he was soon cured.

When Chakravati was about to retire from the Air Force, he told Baba that he would like a job at the ashram. He wanted only to serve the Lord in some capacity, and be near the Divine Feet.

"How can I find a job here for a big officer like you?" Swami teased.

But when the time of his retirement came, Swami appointed him catering officer for the male students' hostel at the Sri Satya Sai College, Whitefield.

It was there that I heard from his lips of the great events that had transformed his life. And there also I met Krishnakishora, then 15 years old and as devoted to Baba as his parents are.

Chakravati introduced him as "Swami's boy," explaining later, "I call him that because without Swami he could never have come to us."

What a fair wind of amazing grace it was that carried the sick and unhappy parachutist into the Field of Divine Compassion back in 1961. There, without his mentioning their sickness, without asking for a cure, both he and his wife were healed immediately. Without a word about their yearning for a child, the barren couple were given a fine son. Above all, perhaps, in a broader sense, the sick parachutist was made whole; in a flash his eyes were opened to a Divine Omnipresence that would henceforth fill his life with spiritual meaning, joy, and contentment.

A Child Shall Lead Them

If you could walk into Swami's Repair Workshop, you might find a notice reading: "What you call a 'miracle' may be done here immediately, or it may take a little time." Following is a case where both time and space were involved.

Early in 1976, in Australia, my wife and I became acquainted with Pearl Harrison, a retired secretary of the medical faculty of a Sydney university. At first we thought this just a chance meeting, but later we wondered.

At the time, the manuscript for my book, *Sai Baba Avatar*, after much rewriting, was ready for the final publisher's draft to be typed cleanly. Pearl, although busy with volunteer welfare work, expressed a desire to type the manuscript. Why she should have this desire she did not understand, but she does now. Anyway, arrangements were made for her to do the typing, and she was introduced to the miracles of Satya Sai Baba.

One of her two granddaughters, 8-year-old Mayan Waynberg, at times would help Pearl's eyes by reading aloud the material to be typed. While the grandmother felt sceptical about the miracles, the granddaughter accepted them without question. To the child they seemed quite natural.

The typing of the first few chapters had been completed when Mayan, who had been looking very pale and was bruising too easily, was taken to a doctor for a blood test. The doctor was appalled at the results. He telephoned Mayan's mother, and strongly advised that the child should be collected from her school and taken home to rest without delay. He also made immediate arrangements for her to be given a bone-marrow test at the Prince of Wales Hospital in Sydney. At this stage the family became very worried, indeed.

Pearl told me about it when I called to find out how the typing was progressing. I could see she was afraid—very afraid—that her little granddaughter might have some drastic killing disease, like leukemia.

It proved not to be leukemia, but something equally drastic and killing—aplastic anemia, in which the bone marrow fails to produce the vital blood components in sufficient quantity to maintain health and life. Her blood picture at that time showed the hemoglobin count at less than half normality, the white components of the blood about a third the normal level, and the platelets way down to one-fifteenth of the normal count.

Mayan was put under the care of a specialist who told her mother that the only treatment was the use of certain drugs—one a male hormone, Prednisolone, and another, Fluoxymesterone. From both of these distressing side effects could be expected, such as stunting the child's growth, causing puffiness and obesity, and bringing hair on the face while causing baldness on the head. The patient would need to have constant blood and bone-marrow tests to monitor her condition. As Mayan had a deep phobia about needles piercing her skin and blood vessels, this was a frightful ordeal for her and everyone else concerned.

But the most tragic part of the situation was that, after going through this treatment and suffering its side effects, she would still not be cured. The best that could be expected was a few more years of life, with very limited activities. The drug therapy was not a cure, the elders were told; all it could do was delay the inevitable for a period. No one could say how long that period would be.

In this sad situation Pearl thought about the Sai miracles she had been typing. She writes: "I must admit to complete lack of faith in religion, considering myself a Jewess by tradition but not by observance. I had typed about many miracles that Sai

Baba had performed, and had thought how interesting it all sounded intellectually, but, had not this dreadful illness occurred to my own granddaughter, I might have let it go at that!

"Then it was as if my mind suddenly opened with a jerk, and I began to think that perhaps there was something real in all I had typed. Howard and Iris Murphet were most concerned when I told them about Mayan. They said they would bring some vibhuti over and Mayan could start taking it immediately."

It has often been said and written that Sai Baba is specially interested in anyone in whom his devotees are interested. So the link was there. Yet, I remembered him saying emphatically that two necessary ingredients of divine healing are faith and surrender. Could we find such ingredients in this Sydney suburban home, where no one seemed to have religious or spiritual interests, and Sai Baba was a remote, almost fictional, figure in a far-off foreign country? Well, we could try.

To Mayan I said earnestly, "You must really and truly believe in the power of Sai Baba."

"Oh, but I *do!*" she replied, and in the way she said it, I sensed the simple child-like faith that Christ had put of first importance.

A little later, Grandfather Jack Harrison made me feel that he, too, may be fertile soil for faith. He said, standing in the garden of their home, "I am going to India as soon as I can to thank Sai Baba for curing Mayan." He did not say "*if* he cures her." The Sai treatment had hardly begun, yet he seemed to have no doubts abouts its effectiveness.

We may be born with faith, that inner certainty of the Omnipotent Supreme, or we may acquire it, but we can never acquire it through reasoning and logic. In fact, the reasoning mind can be a handicap, blocking the birth of the deeper knowledge that men call faith.

Grandmother Pearl had her intellectual barriers but a very warm heart. Mother Helen was noncommittal. Judging by her talk, she was atheistic, but she was willing to try the vibhuti treatment.

We kept assuring the family of the importance of prayer—constant prayer. They agreed to pray to Swami for his help. My wife and I prayed to him fervently and regularly. We badly wanted him to cure Mayan of this shocking disease, not only because we felt love and sympathy for the child, but also because this could be the great Australian miracle that would bring more and more of our fellow countrymen to the light.

There was, however, an urgent question to be answered. We knew from studying many cases that Swami sometimes cures people through drugs prescribed by doctors, while preventing any bad side effects. Sometimes, on the other hand, he will not let drugs be used at all. What would be His Will in the case of Mayan? The only way to be sure was to ask him. In the meantime, we thought, it would be best to let the child start the drug therapy, particularly as the doctors had said that no side effects would become evident for about three months.

We had to find some way of asking Swami the vital question as soon as possible. He must be asked directly, not through any chancy, unreliable telepathy. By good fortune our friend Lynette Penrose was about to set off on a visit to Sai Baba. Incidentally, it had been in Lynette's home in Balmain that we first began Sai meetings in Sydney. I believe they were the first in Australia.

Lynette agreed to take to Swami a photograph of Mayan, and letters asking the vital question about drug treatment. We hoped, moreover, that she would have the opportunity of asking him this question, herself, orally and in person.

She went off to India, and we all eagerly awaited word from her. It was not long before an airmail letter arrived. Lynette told us that she had been granted an interview and had given the photograph and letters to Swami. When he looked at the photograph, she wrote, "his face had become very, very soft and compassionate." About the drug therapy his reply was, "No; no drugs, just vibhuti in water twice a day."

Pearl Harrison writes: "When this message came back, we had to decide whether to take her off the drugs and give her vibhuti only. Mayan made up our minds for us. She said, 'If Sai Baba says I should not take drugs, then I won't take them.' So after just three weeks on the drugs, she went off them and took nothing but vibhuti from then on." This was putting complete faith in the healing power of someone no member of the family had ever seen, except in photographs.

We felt some responsibility as we had been the channel through which they had heard of Sai Baba. All we could do was to hold fast to our own trust and faith in the Lord. Then we thought of something that might help at the receiving end of the Divine Healing Ray. We suggested that they start holding Satya Sai meetings at the Harrison home in Greenacre. They readily agreed to this, and their house on Latvia Street became the second center opened in Sydney for *bhajans* and study.

The meetings were a success from the start, people coming from all parts of the metropolitan area, and from distant places in the Blue Mountains and the south coast. Soon, Jack Harrison decided to convert his large garage into a Sai Temple, buying a new carport to shelter his car. Within the Sai Temple, lined and decorated with the help of devotees, a beautiful shrine was erected. The place acquired a sacred atmosphere and the size of the group expanded.

It was surprising to see, both at the Greenacre Temple and at Balmain, how quickly and wholeheartedly the Australians took to singing bhajans. Many learned to lead, the child Mayan being one of them.

Mayan's health was soon showing a steady improvement. The family decided it might be better to let the doctors think, for the time being, that Mayan was taking their drugs. Every two weeks she was given a blood test at the hospital, and the medical people were delighted at the results. No doubt they were surprised, too. There was a dramatic rise in her red blood cells, a good improvement in the white cells, and the platelet count was creeping upward.

After a few months of the Sai vibhuti treatment, with no medical assistance whatever, the red and white cells were back to normal. The doctors then decided that tests could be taken every two months only, instead of every two weeks as before. Her platelets, in these tests, showed a rise of about 10,000 every two months.

The doctors had earlier examined Mayan's sister, Alona, who is about a year the senior, for bone-marrow compatibility with that of Mayan. When the results were known, and it was found that the sister's bone marrow was compatible, they advised a bone-marrow graft. Even though Mayan's condition was showing satisfactory improvement, the platelets were still far from normal, and it was felt that such a graft would be a help in arresting the disease. Thus another question was posed to the family and to us – should the operation be performed?

Fortunately another Australian devotee, just leaving at this time for Puttaparti, was able to ask Swami directly if the operation should be done or not. Swami's reply was definite: "She is getting better and will soon be completely well. There is no need for such an operation." The news came back to Greenacre quickly, and immediately it was decided – greatly to the relief of Mayan, and indeed all concerned – that there would be no operation. The family felt confident now that nothing was needed but Swami's power, coming through the vibhuti, to bring Mayan's platelets up to normal, and so create a perfectly healthy blood picture.

But though climbing, the platelets were not normal when my wife and I left for India in 1978. However, before we had an opportunity to speak to Swami about the case, we received a letter from Grandmother Pearl, telling us that Mayan's last blood test, given after we left, had shown her platelet count up to normal – in fact, at 174,000, it was better than normal. The child was completely cured of her "incurable" disease.

Early in the next year Jack and Pearl did what he had declared he would do even before the treatment had begun. They came, bringing the two granddaughters, to thank Swami personally for the wonderful, miraculous cure. The family also, at the end, told the specialist in charge of the case that sacred vibhuti had been substituted for the drugs he had prescribed.

He was not as shocked as they had expected. In fact, he said, "I thought it must be something like that as there were no side effects." Then he added, "My mother believes in spiritual healing."

The doctor kindly gave the family all the figures of Mayan's blood tests as documentary evidence. He also agreed to accept a copy of my book, *Sai Baba, Man of Miracles*.

When Pearl handed it to him, she said, "Now, don't let it just lie on the shelf; read it, and then pass it on to somebody else. If you feel you don't want to read it, please send it back to me." It has never come back.

This divine healing across the intervening spaces had worked steadily, taking nearly two years to effect the complete cure. Whatever time factor is involved in such cases has, perhaps, something to do with the receiving end—the particular depth of faith and surrender to God, with the intensity of prayer. There are, no doubt, other inscrutable factors, too; perhaps, for instance, some negative karma to be worked out, or something to be learned from the period of waiting and suffering.

All we can say is, that in moving through hope and prayer and worship toward this great Sai cure, the whole Harrison family—with some relatives and friends as well—moved firmly into the Sai Family. I well remember the day Pearl Harrison broke her intellectual barriers. My wife and I were sitting with Jack and Pearl and the two children, telling some story of Swami's miraculous healing, when suddenly Pearl gave way to a flood of tears. The children, who had never seen their grandmother cry before, were quite alarmed. But Jack understood quite well: "It's the birth of faith," he said. We, who had seen the cool *bhakti* tears on many faces, knew, too, that the mental wall had given way and Pearl had become a devotee. And with the rational mind as an anchor, but not an obstacle, she is, indeed, a very good devotee.

From being without religion, she, and the whole family, have gained a true spiritual religion. Their outlook and values have changed; the joy and love of the Lord fills their lives. While blessing Mayan with a cure of the body, the Divine Hand has touched many other lives for a cure of souls. How pleased and grateful to the Lord my wife and I were that the great Australian miracle had come to pass!

Divine healing touches the vast mystery of life itself. Before healing the man crippled from birth, Jesus said: "Your sins are forgiven." In other words, the cripple's negative karma, up to that point in time, had been wiped out. For without eliminating such karma, how can a karmic disease be removed? Swami has likewise, on several occasions, told people that their slate of past karma had been washed clean. But, of course, if those people go their way making more basic errors, sinning, they will create more bad karma. And bad karma brings disease, in this life or future lives.

A Godman has the power to forgive sins, to rub out the karmic sentences, and thus to cure incurable diseases. But if it is not to a person's highest spiritual interests to remove the karma of suffering, the Godman will not do so. Suffering may be necessary to chisel out deeply engraved karmic tendencies. In such cases the compassionate Lord will cushion the suffering head with his love and tenderness. If possible, he will bring some light of understanding so that the patient knows why he or she must suffer and learns to treat it as a *sadhana* (spiritual discipline). Thus the soul is cured before the body.

While here we are touching only the edge of the great mystery, it is perhaps enough to indicate that in the end we really heal ourselves, as Swami has said.

He is the Guide, the Inspirer, the Divine Catalyst, but it is the High Self, being one with God, that heals the lower self when the essential spiritual lessons have been learned. By understanding this truth, by constantly remembering it, by striving to lead pure lives in loving harmony with our fellow human beings, we gain more and more inner harmony, and in time reach the wholeness where disease is no more.

CHAPTER THREE

Power over Nature

SOLID MATTER DOES not exist. It is a construct of the human senses and mind. What does exist, according to physical science, is a cosmic dance of energy patterns. The power that keeps the cosmic dance going, according to spiritual science, is Divine Mind. The dancing Nataraja of Hindu culture symbolizes this truth.

The important scientific fact for us to note here is that matter is "completely mutable," that is, it can be changed from one appearance to another. The power that created it and sustains it can also change it. That power, Divine Consciousness, is awake in the Avatar, but asleep in you and me.

The present worldview of nature, put forward by high-energy subatomic physics, allows, therefore, for the theoretical possibility of miracles. The fact that they are taking place constantly around Sai Baba has been witnessed by thousands, and can be witnessed by any sceptic who cares to go and see him.

In general, divine miracles reveal the Avatar's nature, and, if we can look deeply enough, teach us something about ourselves. As well as this, each miracle has a particular purpose, connected, perhaps, with compassion, love, the lifting of hearts, the strengthening of faith and devotion, or the calling of people to the spiritual fold. Bhagavan has shown his power over nature in many different ways. Here is a small sample of them.

Power over Distance and Dimension

At the seventh Sri Satya Sai Summer Course in Indian Culture and Spirituality, held at Whitefield in 1979, I met the Convenor of the Course, Professor K. C. Sachdev. One day he told me the story of the ring he wore.

On an occasion when the Professor's wife visited Prasanti Nilayam, Swami materialized a ring for her. She wore this until her death, which happened not long afterward. Then Sachdev decided that—as the gift had been for his wife and not for him—he should return it to Swami.

As soon as possible, as he felt the need of a comforting word from the Lord in his bereavement, he made the trip from his home in the Punjab to see Swami at Prasanti Nilayam. But he forgot to take his late wife's ring, as planned.

He apologized to Swami for this oversight, asking if he should send the ring by post when he returned home.

"No, there's no need for that," Swami said gently. "You keep the ring and wear it yourself."

Sachdev was happy to be told this. As soon as he arrived back home, he took the ring from a drawer. Trying it on, he found that it would not even go over the first knuckle of his little finger. Swami had told him to wear it, but how? Did he mean that Sachdev should wear it on a chain around the neck?

The Professor decided to pray for a sign. Resting the ring on the tip of his third finger, the one on which a wedding ring is usually worn, he placed his palms together in the gesture of prayer. After asking Swami for guidance in this matter, he began to meditate silently.

Some little time later, without thinking what his hands were doing, he must have pressed gently on the ring that was sitting on his finger tip. He came back to normal conscious attention with a start when the ring began to move down his finger. Without hard pressure, it came down over his knuckles to the correct position on his finger. It was a perfect fit.

When he told me the story at Whitefield, the gold ring was still adorning his third finger as if made to measure. In a way it was, for the Lord's love laughs at dimensions, expanding them as required.

Professor Sachdev, a truly humble man, after retiring from his position as President of an educational institute in the north, became a helper in Swami's educational program.

Distance and Atomic Changes

In her home, "Enchanted Acres," Wilma Bronkey has been taking care of crippled and disadvantaged people. The people range from geriatrics to children: in fact, through the many years she has been doing this welfare work, 280 foster children have shared her home.

Then the day came when Sai Baba sent an enchanted call to this woman of compassionate heart. The reason he sent it is known only to himself. The manner in which he sent it to a humble home, 250 miles south of Portland, Oregon, in the United States, would be totally unbelievable to anyone who did not know Sai Baba.

The story came to me from different people—some who knew the lady, and some who had heard the account second-hand. I felt that it may have been highly embroidered in the telling. But when I was finally fortunate enough to meet Wilma Bronkey and hear the story from her own lips, I found that there had been very little embroidery indeed. Some events are so strange, so bizarre in themselves, that our imagination can add nothing to them. Here is the sequence of events as told to me by Wilma Bronkey at Prasanti Nilayam, where extraordinary things are part of the daily norm.

One day at "Enchanted Acres" Wilma answered a long-distance telephone call. A woman's voice said, "Dr. Bronkey, would you please send, as soon as possible, the $200 deposit on your fare to India? Arrangements must be finalized for all those going in Indra Devi's party to see Sai Baba."

Wilma replied, "There must be some mistake. I have no plans to go to India. And who is Sai Baba?"

The line seemed to go dead. There was no further comment, so she hung up. What a strange call, she thought—and why had the voice called her "Doctor" Bronkey? She had no doctorate, but was known generally as the Reverend Bronkey.

She had heard of Indra Devi, a well-known teacher of yoga, and now she felt a strong desire to find out something about Sai Baba. She made some inquiries, and soon the book, *Sai Baba, Man of Miracles*, came into her hands. As she read, she found herself wanting to go to India to see this remarkable man. But she pushed the desire aside. Such a journey was quite impossible for a number of reasons.

Not long after the mysterious telephone call, while she was finding out all she could about Sai Baba, Wilma Bronkey received an honorary doctorate. So, she thought, the voice on the telephone has proved oddly prophetic in one way; will it in another? Nothing seemed to be impossible to Sai Baba. But if he really wanted her to go, he would have to give her an unmistakable sign. Moreover, he would have to remove some difficult obstacles.

Wilma had a great liking for rings and always wore several on her fingers. Among them was a cheap ring with a stone of navy blue, made of glass, and badly scratched with constant wear. But she valued this ring above all the others because it had been a Christmas present from certain of her foster children.

She had formed the habit of taking off all the rings while doing domestic chores, and putting them in a side pocket of her handbag. The reason for this was that, if she went out in a hurry, she could put the rings on at some convenient moment while she was out.

One afternoon Wilma went with a friend to see a film on the care of handicapped people. When it started, she realized that she had seen the same film before, and her interest waned. It was at that time that she noticed she had not put her rings on. She felt in the side pocket of her handbag, resting on the unoccupied seat to her right, and began to slip the rings on her fingers. Then she realized that the one with the dark blue badly scratched stone was missing. Had she put it somewhere else, or had it fallen out of the handbag?

Intently, her mind went back over the events of the day while her eyes rested vaguely on the screen ahead. Then from the corner of her eye she saw a stream of colored sparks flying upward from the handbag at her side. At the same time a strange wind seemed to blow through the theater, and a voice inside her head spoke clearly: "You asked for a sign."

She grabbed the bag and felt carefully inside it. Her fingers contacted the missing ring, but now it felt quite hot. Even in the dim light of the theater it glittered so brightly that the friend by her side exclaimed, "Wow! Where did you get that?"

Excited by the change in the ring's appearance, Wilma hastened out into the foyer to look at it in a brighter light. Her friend came, too. It was the same ring, with the same familiar gold band, but the stone was now a sparkling light blue in color.

Both ladies, highly exhilarated by the incredible happening, left the theater. They were curious to know what kind of stone it was that had taken the place of the dark blue glass. So on the way home they called on a jeweler. Wilma told him she wanted to know the value of the stone for insurance purposes, and handed him the ring. "What a lovely aquamarine!" he exclaimed and, after examining it carefully, valued it at $1,000.

As they continued their drive homeward, the friend protested, "But glass cannot turn into aquamarine. We should ask another jeweler."

They did so. As she handed the ring to him Wilma thought that the shade of blue had changed again. "What is this stone?" she asked. After putting it through some tests, the jeweler told her that it was a sapphire, worth between $1,000 and $1,500.

Wilma thanked him and the ladies returned to their car. "Well, I'm starting to believe in fairies again," remarked the friend, as they drove along. "I wonder if it will change again." Wilma laughed excitedly. No one but Sai Baba could be ringing the changes on the ring to confound the jewelers in this way. "I wonder," she replied. "Let us find another jeweler and see."

They found one. Wilma kept her eyes off the stone as she handed him the ring with a request for its valuation. After examination, he told her it was worth about $1,500.

"And what is the stone?" asked Wilma's friend.

"Oh, a diamond—a nicely cut one," he replied without hesitation. By the time they reached "Enchanted Acres" the stone had returned to the light blue color it had acquired in the theater. And that's the color it was when I saw it on Dr. Bronkey's finger later at Prasanti Nilayam.

The *leela* of the enchanted ring had left Wilma in no doubt that Sai Baba was giving her a sign, and she felt sure that, if he wanted her to go to India, he would remove the obstacles in her way. The two main problems were: who would look after her patients, and how would she get the money for her fare?

The first was solved by her son and daughter-in-law unexpectedly offering to take care of the patients during her absence. The second problem was resolved in an equally unexpected way. Two friends, whom she had once helped with some healing, called to see her. They said, "We know you never take money for healing work, but we feel you really need a sum of money right now. So we want to lend you $2,000. You can take as long as you like to pay it back—and there will be no interest."

That was just the amount she needed, so again the voice on the telephone had proved prophetic. Dr. Bronkey found herself in Indra Devi's party, bound for India and the "Place of Supreme Peace." The day came—the wonderful day—when Wilma Bronkey sat on the sand with the crowd at Prasanti Nilayam, waiting for Swami to appear. He came, floating, it seemed to her, on air. Smoothly he moved around the circle, and eventually stood in front of her. Looking down with a smile, and a merry twinkle in his eyes, he said softly, "How did you like your ring?"

Wilma Bronkey had managed to make several more visits to Swami before the time I met her there at Christmas 1978. She brings parties of sick people for the blessings of the Great Healer. During the 1978 visit, Swami told her to expand her humanitarian work, and to establish a convalescent home for patients who had been cured of cancer.

Dr. Bronkey had been carrying on her fine welfare work for years before the Lord called her in his own amazing way. That call was the milestone of her life. Now behind her service to mankind, blessing it and expanding it, are the love and inspiration of Sai Baba. What that means only those who have experienced it can know.

Beyond Nature and Man

"Street magicians can perform the same tricks as Sai Baba," said a Muslim tailor of Bangalore. "If Baba materialized something never produced by nature or man, I might believe he is what you say he is."

So I told him the story I had just checked about a ring with perpetual motion.

The story first came to me through a young American staying in Bangalore. There might be some mistake in this, thought the sceptic in me; I must try hard to check the facts.

The chance came soon afterward, when I found myself standing next to the bulky figure of Mr. R. Ramanathan Chettiar in Swami's long anteroom at Brindavan, Whitefield.

Mr. Chettiar, the central character of this story, belongs to a family of wealthy jewelers, well known in southern India. Having been a devotee of Sai Baba since about 1946, he has seen many amazing things, and developed a deep veneration for the Avatar he has known personally for so long. His respect and awe are such that he is very loath to talk about the Sai miracles he has experienced without Swami's express permission to do so.

But he realized that his foot of discretion had slipped when I quietly asked if I could see the miracle ring Swami had produced for him, and if it was true that the stone constantly revolved, propelled by some force unknown to man.

"Who told you about it?" he asked, looking quite alarmed.

"I heard it from an American in a hotel in Bangalore."

Apparently realizing that his secret had leaked out and was now spreading in the public domain, he decided to give me the facts, and let me see the object for myself.

One day twelve years earlier Swami had said to him, "As you're a jeweler, I must give you something you can't manufacture for yourself." Whereupon, waving his hand, Baba produced a ring, and slipped it on Chettiar's finger. He has worn it ever since.

It looks much the same as several other rings I have seen come out of the Sai "workshop." The central feature is a beautiful head-and-shoulder portrait of Swami on a circular disc of white enamel, surrounded by a circle of small sparkling stones. The whole is set on a plain gold base, mounted on a gold band of medium thickness. A simple and attractive ring, in which you suspect no magic. Yet the round enamel disc, about one centimeter across, revolves clockwise within the circle of stones, making a complete turn once every twenty-four hours, Mr. Chettiar told me. It had been doing this, he said, without fail, for the twelve years of its existence.

"What about if you take the ring off?" I asked.

"Makes no difference. Sometimes I take it off at night. The center goes on turning just the same."

He kindly removed the ring from his finger to let me examine it more closely. I looked beneath the enamel disc and circle of sparklets. There was nothing there but the plain gold base mounted on the gold band. No room for any mechanism, even if someone had invented a mechanism that would give perpetual motion—which, despite centuries of effort, no one has been able to do. I tried to turn the enamel disc with my finger, but it would not move.

I found it hard to suspect this solid citizen, who looked so sane and honest, of inventing such a fantastic story. What possible motive could he have for doing so? Yet I felt I must check for myself to see if the centerpiece did actually revolve.

As if he read my thoughts, Mr. Chettiar said, "You see where Swami's head is pointing now." If the circle had been a clockface, the head would be pointing to about two o'clock, I noted. "Well," he went on, "look at it again when we come to afternoon darshan."

It was about six hours later when we met again in the room, and I asked to see the ring. Swami's head now pointed downward to about five o'clock. It had traveled through a quarter of the circle in the six hours, which indicated that it would do the complete turn in twenty-four hours—as the earth rotates on its axis.

As both Mr. Chettiar and I were staying in cottages within the Brindavan grounds, I had no difficulty in seeing him several times a day as we went to and from Baba's residence. Each time I saw him, I made a point of asking permission to examine the ring again. Thus, by noting the position of the portrait's head, I was able to establish beyond doubt that the disc of enamel made a complete revolution every twenty-four hours.

"Are the small stones around the circumference valuable?" I once asked him.

"Not commercially. But it is a blessed ring, and therefore priceless."

As well as being blessed and unique, it seemed to be a charmed ring in another way. Although Mr. Chettiar had worn it for twelve years, there was not a mark or scratch on it. By contrast the enamel centerpiece of my own Sai-produced ring, though then only about four years old, was badly scratched and worn. Even if the wealthy jeweler never did any manual work—which I often do—no ordinary ring could look so new after twelve years of constant use.

After I had told this story to the Muslim tailor, he said, "If three scientists took the ring and locked it away in a safety vault, and together examined it several times a day for many days, and found that it did revolve, I might believe it."

This remark did nothing to relieve my annoyance with him over the bad job he had made of a pair of trousers. But later I thought — well, why should he believe me anyway? Why, for that matter, should he believe three scientists, or thirty scientists? Such incredible powers over matter and energy have to be seen personally to be believed — by most people.

There are two postscripts to this story. The first is that, about a week after telling it, I received a letter at Prasanti Nilayam from the Bangalore tailor. He wrote that, on the night following our conversation, he had had a darshan of Sai Baba in a dream, and now he realized that he had been mistaken, and that Baba's powers are genuine. Could I let him know Swami's movements as he wished to take some friends to Whitefield after Baba returned there? The second postscript spins another strand in Swami's web of inscrutability. A few months after Mr. Chettiar kindly told me the story of his revolving ring, I happened to meet him again. In the interim one or the other of us had been absent from the group around Swami, and we had not seen each other.

After greeting him, I inquired if the wonderful ring was still rotating steadily in rhythm with the earth on its axis.

"No," he replied. "One day, a few weeks after I told you about it, Swami said, 'That ring has been turning long enough.' He took it in his hand, blew on it, and returned it to me. It has not revolved since."

"Did he give any reason for stopping it?"

"No — only that it had gone on long enough."

There must have been a reason for both the beginning and the end of this strange leela, but neither of us understood what it was.

Divine Alchemy

Several people who have known Baba, and traveled with him for many years, have told me that they have witnessed him transmute water into petrol. He does not do this normally, and is not attempting to solve the world energy crisis this way. As he has often said, he will not interfere with nature on a large scale. Divine alchemy is used only on rare occasions under particular circumstances—as when Jesus turned water to wine at Cana in Galilee, and Moses turned the waters of the Nile to blood in Egypt.

An old Sai devotee told me that, just after the Second World War, he was in a car with Swami and others driving through the countryside. They were on their way to an important religious festival, and did not want to be late. Suddenly, in the middle of nowhere, their car ran out of petrol. One of the passengers, who knew the district, thought there was a service station about three miles up the road, but, as petrol was not plentiful at that time, there may not be any available there.

The driver said he would walk to the service station, or somewhere, and try to get a can of petrol. But even if he managed to secure some, this would mean a considerable delay. Also it was a long, hard walk for the man on a hot day; and, though he was at fault for not having ensured that there was enough petrol in the tank at the start of the journey, Swami was merciful.

He said to the driver, "Bring a bucket of water from that house. There's a well there." He pointed to a humble dwelling less than a hundred meters away.

The driver obeyed silently. Everyone remained silent in a kind of hushed expectancy as they stood waiting with Swami beside the car.

Soon the driver returned with a large pail full of water. "Here," Swami indicated, and the driver placed the pail on the ground at the Lord's feet. All watched intently as the red robed figure leaned over and with one finger stirred the surface of the water.

"Put it in the petrol tank—and be careful not to spill any," he told the driver.

Soon they were driving along again as the engine drank the miracle petrol happily; they reached the religious festival in good time.

There is evidence, moreover, that the divine finger will stretch many thousands of miles to stir petrol into being. A pleasant-mannered, turbaned Punjabi, named Surjitsingh Chahal, told me many strange things when I met him once on the grounds of Brindavan, Whitefield. Finally, he gave me a letter he had received from a friend, a Mr. Gordon Chetty of Durban, South Africa. In this Mr. Chetty writes: "I have a 1970 model, nine-seater station wagon which I use to travel to any destination to spread Bhagavan Baba's teachings. Bhagavan started providing petrol miraculously for this vehicle. This has happened eleven times in two years. Each time the miracle has been witnessed by hundreds of people. It happens like this: while the vehicle is standing stationary, the tank fills to overflowing, and a quantity of petrol often pours from the mouth. Many people have, in fact, placed containers in position to collect the overflow.

"One Sunday morning, for instance, I was at a wedding party. I had left my vehicle parked on the roadside among other cars. It was about 11:30 in the morning when I was called urgently, and told to go to my station wagon as petrol was spilling from it. I found that the petrol tank had filled up completely and was overflowing. Many people from the wedding party rushed out to see this miracle. There were, in fact, about eight hundred witnesses that time. Twelve people collected petrol from the overflow to use in their own vehicles.

"We have seen many other Baba miracles here—such as instant healing in the Sai Baba shrine in our home. Many have been directed to this shrine by Baba in dreams. Leaking hearts, rheumatic hearts, and cancer are among the diseases cured here by the grace of Bhagavan."

Although Swami, in other cases, transmuted water into petrol, in Durban he seems to have multiplied the petrol that was already in the tank. The help and grace of the Lord comes where and in the manner that he himself prescribes.

Teleports (Apports)

In 1961, before we had even heard of Sai Baba, or had any intention of visiting India, my wife and I were staying in England for a time. Part of the time we spent at the home of my wife's Uncle Clarry, who was a non-professional medium. For years he had acted in this capacity to please a group of friends who met once a week in a private home. We attended several of these spiritualist meetings during our visit, driving with Uncle Clarry and his wife and daughter, the few miles from their home to the meeting place in Southport.

At one of the meetings a phenomenon took place that I want to describe here. There were perhaps six or seven people present besides our two selves, the medium and his family. We sat as usual in a rather small room with the blinds drawn to keep out the street lights. The electric light in the room was switched off, and, in the darkness, everyone in the circle sang hymns. Sometimes Uncle Clarry requested a particular hymn. After this had gone on for about ten minutes, we could hear by the medium's deep breathing that he was in a trance. Then the singing stopped and we all sat in silence, awaiting any message that might come.

Such messages usually came by a voice speaking through a light metal trumpet that had been placed, before the lights went out, on the carpet in the middle of the circle. As Uncle Clarry was a direct-voice medium, these disembodied voices would sound from any point in the room, often high up near the ceiling.

The first voice that spoke on this particular night told us that there would be very little communication that night, as those on "the other side" were going to attempt a special phenomenon that would take most of the power available. Chitchat between the living and the so-called dead being the usual practice at the séances, I looked forward with keen interest to any other type of phenomenon that might take place.

Presently, a voice addressed me, telling me to cup my two hands together for receiving a teleport. I did as told. After a pause there was a peculiar rattling noise which appeared to come from the trumpet high in the air above me. Then it came closer and I felt a small object drop into my cupped palms. It was hard and round and seemed to be covered with something that felt like wet salt. What can it be, I wondered in the darkness. Well, I would know when the light came on. I put it in my jacket pocket.

Meantime I hoped for a clue from the trumpet, but all the voice said was: "This has been brought to you from a country where you have no intention of going, but you will go there and be very happy. The object is from a holy place in that country, and you will see more like it when you go there." Then there was silence; the trumpet fell to the floor; the room seemed empty, and soon the meeting was closed.

The object had lost its wet, salty feel, and was quite dry when I took it out of my pocket to look at it in the light. It was a smooth, brown pebble, about an inch in diameter.

In conversation next day I asked Uncle Carry where it had come from. But he had no idea. The first time he had seen it, or known of its existence, was when he came out of his trance at the meeting. After a silence, he said, "The word 'Ganges' comes to my mind. Does that mean anything to you?"

"I know it's a river in India, that's all," I answered.

Uncle Clarry never took any money for his mediumistic services and his only motive for carrying them on was to keep his friends happy. He had no reason for cheating anyone.

Even if he had wanted to play some joke on me, I thought, he could not have carried a wet pebble in his pocket all the way from his home to the meeting room and kept it there, still wet, until the time when it dropped into my hands—about an hour altogether. Why, within five minutes in my pocket the pebble had dried completely, and the material clinging to it had rubbed off!

So whether the pebble had come from a riverbed in some distant country, or from somewhere in England, it had arrived in my hands as it had left its location – coated with wet sand or soil. I kept the stone, hoping some day to solve its mystery.

A "chance" conversation with someone in London made us decide to go to India in 1964 to attend a six-months' course on the Ancient Wisdom at the headquarters of the Theosophical Society. At the end of the course we journeyed to the north of India in search of spiritual teachings. Among the places we visited were some ashrams at Rishikesh along the sacred River Ganges.

One day while we were strolling along the banks of the river, we saw some piles of brown pebbles lying in the wet sand on the edge of the riverbed. Something made me pick up one of the pebbles; it was lightly coated with wet sand, and the feel of it made me think of the apport that had come into my hands in England.

Knowing that the apported pebble was lying at the bottom of my suitcase back at the Sivananda Ashram, I put the stone from the river in my pocket and we returned to the ashram to make a comparison. By the time I took it out of my pocket, about half an hour later, the pebble was quite dry and smooth. The two pebbles were very similar in appearance.

Then the prophecies came back to my mind. The disembodied voice had said that the apport was from a holy place in a country we would visit and find great happiness there. Then the word "Ganges" had come clairaudiently into Uncle Clarry's mind, and the Ganges is certainly a holy river to all Hindus. Also the area of Rishikesh, itself, has a sacred atmosphere. We had had no intention of visiting India when we were sitting that evening in a spiritualist circle in the north of England three years earlier. Now here we were in that country, very happy because it seemed to be our spiritual home.

Soon after that, when we came to Sai Baba, our happiness in Bharat (sacred India) increased immeasurably. Strange as it may seem, and unbelievable to some people, I have little doubt that the brown pebble, that even now lies on the desk before me, was teleported in a flash from the sands of the Ganges to that sitting room in Southport, England. Outside of space and time, it came as a prophecy and forerunner of the greatest event of our lives.

While this kind of phenomenon by discarnate entities usually, but not always, requires conditions of darkness, there are many examples of it being performed in daylight by great yogins. The psycho-kinetic (PK) power, inherent in all of us, manifests itself through prolonged yogic disciplines.

For instance, in his book, *Living with the Himalayan Masters,* Swami Rama tells how once, while he was in Tibet with his Grandmaster, he felt a strong wish that he had brought his diary with him to record his experiences. He had actually left the diary behind in India at "a sanitarium called Bhuwali, near the Nainital Hills."

Reading his pupil's thoughts, the Grandmaster said, "I can get your diary for you. Do you need it?" "Yes, and a few pencils, too," replied Swami Rama.

His diary was quite large, containing 475 pages, but within seconds it was lying there before him, with three pencils beside it.

For some odd reason, which I cannot understand, there are devotees of Sai Baba who declare that he does not teleport, or apport, things. The implication is that all his miraculous productions are new creations. This is hardly a tenable theory when he often says, himself, that he will "get" something from somewhere—and at times, when necessary, he sends the item back to where it came from.

An instance of his getting something from a distance—and happily not sending it back—was when, at Horsley Hills in 1967, he teleported a coin for me.[1] On that occasion he said, after inquiring the year of my birth, "I will get you a coin made in America that year." When it came into his hand, and he passed

---

[1] See *Sai Baba: Man of Miracles* by Howard Murphet (York Beach, ME: Samuel Weiser, 1992), p. 84.

it to me, he said, "It is no longer in circulation, otherwise I would not give it to you."

It was a ten-dollar gold piece, and some years later a coin expert in America confirmed that it was a genuine coin minted in San Francisco in 1906, the year of my birth.

An incident in which Swami brought an item for sighting, and then sent it back, is reported by Mr. N. Kasturi in his writings on the life of Sri Satya Sai Baba.[2]

It took place at Kanya Kumari (Cape Comorin) in 1958. At the time it happened, Baba was sitting on the beach with a small group of devotees. One of the devotees had been reading a book about the pilgrim center there, and Baba asked him what it said about the temple. The devotee then told the story of a diamond that had once adorned the nose-stud of the temple goddess. It was such a magnificent diamond, the book said, that pirates could see it shining out at sea. So, one day they raided the temple and carried off the diamond. Its subsequent fate was not known to the writer of the book.

After hearing the story to its end, Baba said, "Do you want to see that diamond? I know exactly where it is now. I can bring it for you to see and send it back before its absence is noticed."

All agreed eagerly that they would like to see the famous diamond, whereupon Baba simply patted the sand in front of him, and suddenly there was the glittering diamond! He held it up for everyone to see clearly, and then it simply vanished from his hand. What was that, I wonder, if not a teleport?

I have no doubt that teleports form part of the broad spectrum of Swami's powers over nature, which includes changing the shape and size of objects, harnessing new energies not known to science, transmuting one form of matter into another, transcending time and space, multiplying the quantity of a substance and creating new material objects from the mutable parti-

---

[2] See *The Life of Bhagavan Sri Satya Sai Baba* by N. Kasturi (Puttaparthi, India: Prasnthi Nilayam Press, n.d.).

cles and energy patterns of the universe. As we shall see in later chapters, he also has the power to change his own form and to multiply forms of himself.

CHAPTER FOUR

The Sai Forms

A T THIS PERIOD of history God is, I believe, using certain Sai forms to raise human beings to higher levels of awareness. First there was the Sai Baba who was born last century in the hamlet of Patri on the River Godàvari, but lived most of his life in the village of Shirdi. Now there is Satya Sai Baba, who was born in Puttaparti on the River Chitravati, eight years after the old Shirdi form was cast off. Finally, Satya Sai states, there will be Prema Sai who, one year after the passing of the Satya Sai form, will be born in Karnataka (the old Mysore state), at a place between Bangalore and the city of Mysore.

Does the name "Sai Baba" have any significance, and if so, what? "Baba" is a well known appellation for "father"; but "Sai" is not so easy to define. Some have said that it is an old Persian word for "saint." But one deeper meaning of "Sai" is "mother"–Satya Sai points out. The whole name then means "mother-father," and undoubtedly to his devotees Swami is the Divine Mother-Father figure.

In the spiritual lore of Hinduism, however, we find a further meaning for the word "Sai." The Bauls, a sect of mendicant devotees of Vishnu, give the name to one who has reached perfection. They say, "No one is greater than a Sai. The Sai is a man of supreme perfection who does not see any differentiation in the world."[1]

The name "Sai Baba" began to be known in the last quarter of last century when a young mendicant told the inhabitants of the village of Shirdi that his name was Sai Baba. It was used thereafter by the gathering stream of his followers.

Then at the age of 14, after he had gone through a profound psychic experience, Satyanarayana Raju of Puttaparti announced to the "gazing rustics ranged around" that he was Sai Baba. The name sounded suspiciously Moslem to Hindu village ears.

Perhaps all the meanings given are applicable. "Sai" is a saint, a divine mother, and, as the God-intoxicated devotees of Vishnu understand it, a man of supreme perfection, so united with God that in the multiplicity of this world he sees only the one formless, undifferentiated Divine.

Though walking the earth now in the temporal form of Satya Sai, the Lord nevertheless shows himself at times in the old form of Shirdi Sai. Yesterday, today, tomorrow being equally within his omniscience, I feel sure he could manifest as Prema Sai as well. But as that form is not known, there would be no point in doing so. He did, however, as a matter of interest, manifest for John Hislop a ring bearing the profile of Prema Sai.

Why he sometimes appears as Shirdi Sai is a mystery. Mostly the people concerned do not themselves understand the reason for it.

There is, for instance, Maria Viljacik, a Sai devotee living near Wollongong in New South Wales, Australia. Maria's first contact with Sai Baba was when she was a child, living in Yugoslavia. In those years she used to have visits from an old man who she thought was a beggar. Usually she was terrified of beggars, she says, but strangely had no fear of this particular one. He would suddenly appear, then sit and talk to her, giving her

---

[1] *The Gospel of Sri Ramakrishna,* translated by Swami Nikhilananda (Hollywood, CA: Vedanta Press, n.d.), p. 471.

advice, and helping her with her childhood problems. A love for
the old man grew in her heart, and she often wondered who he
was and where he came from.

Many years later, after she had come with her husband and
daughter to live in Australia, Maria saw a picture of Shirdi Sai
and with a shock realized that she was looking at the beloved
old beggar of her childhood. She became very eager to find out
more about him.

Soon afterward, through an Indian who came to live for a
time at Wollongong, she heard about Shirdi Sai's reincarnation
as Satya Sai, and learned to her great joy that there were regular
Sai Baba meetings in Sydney. Though these meetings, for bhajans and discussions, were some fifty miles away from her home,
Maria and her husband and daughter began attending them
regularly.

The daughter, Veronica, who was a musician, soon became
one of the bhajan leaders. Her devotional feelings were so strong
that she used to get up at about four o'clock every morning and
sing bhajans alone in the dark of her small music room until
daybreak.

When my wife and I went to India to see Swami in January
1978, we took photographs of the Viljacik family, music composed to Baba by Veronica, and some essays the young woman
had written on spiritual themes. As we presented these things to
Swami, I mentioned Maria's childhood experiences. "Yes," he
said, "she is an old devotee."

Toward the end of 1978, Maria and her husband, Andy,
came to India for Swami's darshan. Iris and I accompanied them
from their hotel in Bangalore to Whitefield, and Swami told us
to bring them inside for an interview. He talked to them of their
lives and problems, filling them with great happiness. Then the
following day, at a second interview, he materialized a beautiful
ring for Maria.

She was so overcome with awe and reverence for the ring
that, unlike most people who like to display such things, she
kept it hidden as she walked through the curious crowd outside
Swami's house.

Maria herself does not know why the Lord came to her first as Shirdi Sai, though she does retain a great love for that form, while readily accepting the new form as the same Sai Baba.

There are still some people, however, who do not accept Satya Sai as a reincarnation of Shirdi Sai. Swami says that they are stuck with the old form—and he does not want us to be stuck with any form. Yet even highly educated and devout people can fall into the fatal error of worshiping the form rather than the God beyond it.

Here is a story related by Mr. Justice S. Suryamurthy, Judge in the High Court of Madras. The strange event he describes took place several years ago when he was "at another station." The lady in the story, whose name is not given for obvious reasons, was the headmistress of a college for women.

The Judge writes: "My neighbor was a lady educationist. One evening she came to my house and found pictures of Sri Satya Sai Baba in the entrance to the hall. She turned around and asked me, 'Do you believe in this rowdy?'

"Sensing her militant mood, and to avoid a controversy with her, I said merely that a friend had given these pictures to me, and I had had them hung on the wall. She began telling me that she is a devotee of Shirdi Sai, and performs her *puja* every Thursday. She also abused Sri Satya Sai.

"I was at that time merely a half-hearted devotee of Sri Satya Sai, and did not react violently to her attack. After declaiming to her heart's content, the lady left.

"A couple of days later, which was a Thursday, I returned home late in the evening. I was surprised to find the same lady waiting in my house. The moment I entered, she began to tell me something, gasping for breath as she spoke. This was what she told me.

"Earlier the same evening she had gone to her puja room, as usual on Thursdays. She had lifted the idol of Shirdi Sai and begun anointing it when the puja room door opened and Sri Satya Sai entered. Suspecting that I had brought Him there, and enraged at His entering her puja room without permission, she attempted to reprimand Him.

"But she could not open her mouth. Nor would her limbs move. She sat as if fixed to the place, unable even to stand up. Baba went and sat on a chair in the room. He told her that He and 'the old fellow' (referring to Shirdi Sai Baba) are one. He asked her, 'Why do you abuse me?' Then, even as He was sitting on the chair, His figure faded away. Her limbs were released and she was able to stand up.

"She realized that it had been a vision, and rushed at once to my house to tell me about it. Not finding me there, she had waited until I returned home."

The Judge does not say if the lady afterward became a devotee of the Satya Sai form. But one can well imagine, from her reaction to the vision, that she must have been shaken out of her fixed addiction to the Shirdi Sai form, and her violent prejudice against Sri Satya Sai.

I am very grateful to Judge Suryamurthy for giving me his written testimony of an event that confirms dramatically Swami's omniscience and power to project his form wherever necessary in the interests of Truth, and the understanding and welfare of his devotees.

Through many years of association with Bhagavan Satya Sai Baba and his leading devotees, I have long ago accepted the identity of Satya Sai and Shirdi Sai. The factors contributing to this acceptance are too numerous and subtle to set forth and elucidate here, but not the least among them is a study of the life and teachings of Shirdi Sai. Then if one also studies the life and teachings of Satya Sai, one can have no doubt that he and "the old fellow" are one.

But for the benefit of readers who have not had this cumulative experience, I will relay another story—one told me by the eminent scientist and Sai devotee, Dr. S. Bhagavantam. He told it during a car journey from Puttaparti in 1979.

"Nearly twenty years ago," he said, "when I was quite a new devotee, I went to a place in Trivandrum where a lot of people had gathered to see Swami. I was standing near him, among other people, when I heard him say, referring to an old lady across the room, 'I knew that woman when she was only a baby.'

"My mind began to question how such a thing was possible, and after a while I said to him, 'But, Swami, that woman must be 70 years old, while you are just over 30, so how could you have known her when she was a baby?' 'I knew her in my former life at Shirdi,' he replied.

"Well, I was, as I said, only a new devotee, and one that liked to question and test everything. The scientist in me was still very active, even though I had seen many things inexplicable to science. Today I would take Bhagavan's word for it, but then I needed to check on what he said.

"After a time I made the opportunity by moving near to the old lady in question and engaging her in conversation. I asked her if she had ever been to Shirdi. She replied that her uncle had taken her there when she was a small child. In fact, Shirdi Sai had produced a locket for her, she said, and she still wore it. She held it up for me to see.

"The whole incident was a profoundly moving experience for me. On top of other things, it convinced me that the two Sais were one and the same."

Occultism teaches that the occupation of the body by the reincarnating entity does not take place completely at either conception or birth. It comes about in stages through early life. Moreover, even at maturity, when there is the greatest integration, the total individual soul is not fully immersed in the body. In fact, it is never fully immersed.

This must be more emphatically true of an Avatar. Shirdi Sai used to say, "Do not make the mistake of thinking that I am this 3½ cubits (approximately 6' 3") of body." The body is merely the earthly focus of something infinitely greater.

It is reasonable to suppose that when Sai Baba dropped the 3½ cubits, and took for himself another, much shorter body, he did not come fully into the new physical vehicle, with all his powers, until it had been developed sufficiently for his use.

The following experience of an old Shirdi Sai devotee suggests that this was so, and provides more evidence, for the doubter, that the two Sai Babas are one.

His Holiness Gayathri Swami had spent a year with Sai Baba at Shirdi in 1906, and then had visited him frequently until Shirdi Sai cast off his body in 1918. Some forty years later, His Holiness went to Prasanti Nilayam to see his old guru's reincarnation as Satya Sai.

While there, he related to people at the ashram many anecdotes about life at Shirdi. It is always delightful to hear such anecdotes, and to realize how they echo many things that take place at Puttaparti now. Even some of the jokes made by Sai Baba at Shirdi are repeated in this incarnation.

But Gayathri Swami's most impressive experience took place the night before he left Prasanti Nilayam. During that night he had a vision in which Sai Baba appeared in the old Shirdi form and told his devotee that he had left his mahasamadhi after eight years, and had brought all his properties fifteen years later.

H. H. Gayathri Swami did not know at the time of this vision that Satya Sai Baba was born eight years after the death (mahasamadhi) of Shirdi Sai. Nor did he know that the youth Satyanarayana Raju had assumed the name "Sai Baba," and had begun manifesting all the powers of Shirdi Sai, following a profound psychic experience some fifteen years after the conception of the new incarnation.

He was told these biographical facts by friends at Prasanti Nilayam after he had described his vision to them. Then he understood, he said, what the Shirdi Sai vision had meant by "his properties"—they were his powers.

The gentle old swami went away happily convinced that his Shirdi Sai sadguru was back on earth as Satya Sai Baba of Puttaparti.[2]

There are many stories telling of Swami being in more than one place at the same time. Nagamani Purnaiya, who first went to Baba in 1945, knew of several such events. Here is one from

---

[2] This story is related by N. Kasturi in his *The Life of Bhagavan Sri Satya Sai Baba*, Vol. 1.

her privately printed book, *The Divine Leelas of Bhagavan Sri Satya Sai Baba.*

> I have written in earlier books about Leela Mudaliar, a professor of botany in Madras, who is also in charge of the Guindy Temple, which her late father dedicated to Shirdi Sai Baba.

> Nagamani Purnaiya relates how one year Leela Mudaliar came to Puttaparti and asked Swamiji to attend the *akhanda bhajan* which she would shortly be celebrating at the Guindy Temple in Madras. Swami promised to do so.

> She sent out printed invitations and many devotees arrived expecting to see Swami there. But there was no sign of him and, after waiting a long time, Leela at last gave up and went to light the lamp to begin. At that moment Swami arrived and the 24-hour akhanda bhajan began in his presence. Swami was still at Guindy next morning, and did the ritual of *mahamangalaarati*. At twelve o'clock Swami had lunch, blessed all the people there, and went away.

> Leela wrote a letter to a friend in Puttaparti describing the event, and saying how happy they all were that Swami had spent so much time with them. The friend was greatly puzzled because Swami had been in Puttaparti all that time. She wrote to Leela, saying that there must be some mistake because it had been a festival day at Puttaparti on that akhanda bhajan day, and Swamiji had been there all the time, so he could not have been in Madras.

> But Leela knew that he certainly was in Madras; many had been at the Temple and seen him and even touched

[3] Nagamani Purnaiya, *The Divine Leelas of Bhagavan Sri Satya Sai Baba.* Self-published in 1969, Bangalore, India.

his feet. Yet many had seen him at Puttaparti, too. In the end they came to the conclusion that Swami had been in both places at the same time—not just briefly, but for a long period, making crowds of devotees happy in Madras, while doing the same in Puttaparti.

"God can do many wonders," Nagamani Purnaiya concludes.

Even some great saints of the past have been capable of bi-location. The Krishnavatara multiplied his form many times to partner each gopi in the rasa dance. So why should we doubt that the Sai Avatara could also manifest as many forms for himself as required at any one time, imbuing each form with divine consciousness, and, if necessary, solidifying any of them to give the impression of physical presence? He is the Master of Form— physical or subtle.

CHAPTER FIVE

Using Other Forms

SATYA SAI BABA sometimes changes his form temporarily, not only to the Shirdi Sai appearance, but to something quite different. Why does he choose different appearances under different circumstances? There are, no doubt, very good reasons, though they may lie beyond our human understanding. Let us look at a few examples of such amazing, and often dramatic, changes.

In recent years an old, ardent devotee was driving to Ootacamund (Ooty) alone with his driver on a visit to Swami who was staying there. It was nighttime and the driver became lost. The devotee, who had not been concentrating on their route, had no idea of their location, but he felt that they were going in the wrong direction.

They stopped and considered whether they should go back or go forward until they found some signpost. There was a good moon, which would help them. Suddenly, while they were talking, a man appeared beside the car. He was riding a motorcycle and, to the devotee's surprise, was wearing silk. This much he could see in the moonlight, though the color of the flowing silk clothes was not completely discernible.

Asking if he could help, and being told of their dilemma, the motorcyclist told them to turn around and return to the first crossroads; and he gave clear directions on how they should proceed after that. Then he rode off and vanished quickly – too quickly, the devotee thought.

Following the rider's directions, they soon reached their destination. When, shortly after his arrival, the devotee came into Swami's presence, the latter remarked casually, "You took the wrong road. I sent someone to help you." Was the phantom rider Swami himself? The old devotee thinks so.

When Swami travels by car between Whitefield and Puttaparti, or from Whitefield to Madras, there is usually a procession of devotees' cars following him. For example, when I was fortunate enough to accompany him in his car from Whitefield to Puttaparti near Christmastime in 1978, I counted eleven cars following us.

On one occasion, on the road from Whitefield to Madras, a car in the middle of a long Sai convoy broke down. The vehicles following it stopped and between them took the passengers of the disabled car on to Madras. The owner, who had been driving the car himself, said he would stay with the vehicle, and asked one of his friends to send a mechanic back from the first garage along the road. He knew that would be many miles away, but he had no understanding of motor engines, himself, so he sat down for a long wait.

The summer heat of midday was very oppressive in the stationary car, and he was about to walk to the shade of a tree some fifty yards back along the road, when he saw a lone cyclist riding toward him. This was surprising because the cyclist was coming from the direction of Whitefield, and he knew that he had not passed anyone on a bike for many miles.

The cyclist stopped and asked if he could be of any help.

"Not unless you know a mechanic somewhere nearby."

"I'm a mechanic, myself," the cyclist said, walking over and opening the hood of the car.

Within seconds he announced, "Your fan belt is broken." Then, to the devotee's amazement, and relief, he took from his pocket a new fan belt of the right type and size to fit the car's engine. After fixing it in place, the cyclist continued his journey, refusing to take any money for his labor.

Grateful for this stroke of good fortune, the devotee soon started his engine and drove on toward Madras. The cyclist had gone round a bend in the road just ahead, and the devotee decided to stop, when he caught up with him, and try again to pay him, or perhaps offer him a lift. They could tie his bike on the roof rack, on top of the suitcases already there.

But when he drove round the turn, the road stretching for miles ahead was quite empty. The cyclist had vanished into the shimmering air.

The devotee arrived in Madras and made straight for the house where he knew Swami would be staying. Parking his car in the street, he went inside and slipped quietly into the room where he could hear Swami's voice talking to a group of people. As he moved forward diffidently, hopeful of touching the Divine Feet, Swami smiled a welcome and said, "So your car broke down. I sent someone along to help you."

As well as taking different mundane forms, Baba has assumed various traditional Divine Appearances at different times. To some people he has shown himself as Jesus Christ, to others as Subramaniam, as Krishna, as Rama, to one couple as the Goddess Lakshmi, and so on. It often depends on the occasion and the *Ishtthadevata,* or particular divine form, customarily worshipped by the person or people concerned. In this way Baba demonstrates the lesson he is constantly teaching in words—that God can take any form, yet it is ever the One and Only God.

If human beings could have understood and accepted this vedantic truth in the past, the religious wars and persecutions would surely not have taken place. All religions could have co-existed in mutual tolerance and harmony.

I will now describe events in which Swami has taken specific Divine Forms to the eyes of different devotees, at the same time demonstrating other divine powers and understanding.

Rama

Lord Rama was the *Ishtthadevata* of the late Raja of Venkatagiri, though members of his family worshipped other divine forms.

Each respected the other's personal preferences in the matter of the divine cloaks that the One God wears.

The Raja, when he first met young Satya Sai, felt sure he was an Avatar, and always treated him with profound veneration. He begged the Avatar to honor his palace by spending some time there. Swami agreed to pay the visit, and a suitable time was arranged.

His eldest son being away when the time for Swami's visit drew near, the Raja asked his younger son, Gopal, to take the big palace car and bring Swami from Puttaparti.

Gopal, however, begged leave to decline. As he told me years later, his only interest at the time was cricket, which he played for his state, Andhra Pradesh. He felt no interest whatever in Sai Baba or any other spiritual figure.

That night he dreamed a dream in which Swami came to him and gave him two mangoes to eat. After he had eaten them, he awoke with a tremendous urge to go to Puttaparti. Though it was the middle of the night, he jumped out of bed and went to tell his father about his sudden change of mind. The old Raja did not mind being awakened to hear this surprising news.

Next day he gave Gopal certain instructions about the journey, one of them being to send a telegram on the day he was leaving Puttaparti with Swami; then from every main center he passed through on the route home, he was to send another telegram. Thus the Raja would be kept informed of the Avatar's progress toward Venkatagiri, and the expected time of his arrival there.

The Raja's intention was to meet the palace car outside the gates and bring Sai Baba through the town of Venkatagiri in royal procession. It was to be a reception with all the pageantry and trappings fit for a king. Gopal promised faithfully to send all the telegrams as instructed, and set off on the long journey over rough roads to the remote, little known village of Puttaparti.

In those early days, Gopal told me, the road stopped on the banks of the River Chitravati opposite Puttaparti. Passengers had to wade across the narrow stream that flowed through the broad sands of the riverbed. When Gopal arrived, he saw

Swami on the sands and quickly waded across to him. As they met, Swami smiled a welcome and remarked, "They must have been powerful mangoes you ate."

A glory seemed to shine around the young Swami and Gopal could not say anything. Baba patted him affectionately, and went on, "We will leave for Venkatagiri in two or three days."

Gopal's interest in cricket took second place from that time on. Though Sai Baba was only about his own age, and village-born, he seemed to know everything, and was completely in command of every situation.

When, after a few days at Puttaparti, they were about to leave, Gopal remembered his father's instructions about the telegrams, and told Swami.

"There will be no need for that," Sai Baba smiled.

Gopal never disobeyed his father, but Swami was so much in control, emanating such confidence and power, that Gopal felt everything would be all right, and forgot his father's request.

Even so, as they approached Venkatagiri, he was somewhat surprised and relieved to see his father and a crowd waiting outside the gates to receive them.

When, at the head of his relatives and retainers, the Raja stepped forward to greet the visitor, instead of Sai Baba, he saw Lord Rama sitting there in the palace car. Then his joy knew no bounds, and he took the Avatar in procession to the palace.

Later, in a quiet moment, Gopal asked his father how he had known what time the car would be arriving.

"I knew by your telegrams, of course," the Raja replied.

"But . . . but, I didn't send any telegrams. Sai Baba wouldn't let me."

"What are you talking about? Did not send any?"

The Raja picked up several telegrams and showed them to his son. They all bore Gopal's name as the sender. Gopal shook his head in bewilderment. "And yet I did not send any," he insisted.

The Raja was impressed by his son's manner and began to feel that something strange had happened. He remembered that each telegram had appeared on a table while he was out of the room, and he had thought that a servant had taken them from the post office messenger, and placed them there. Now he wondered.

He sent for the postmaster, and asked if any telegrams had been received, addressed to the Raja, and delivered to the palace that day.

"No, none," was the reply.

Then the Raja understood, and Gopal began to understand, that the telegrams had been "precipitated" into the palace by the power of Sai Rama.

Gopal, unlike his father and elder brother, had not bothered to study the great Hindu scriptures, but he began now to worship Sai Baba as an embodiment of the Divine. This spiritual perception and understanding were enhanced by many things that happened through the years following that miracle journey when the Lord first rode beside him to his ancestral home.

"Now I have two interests in life—Swami and cricket," he told me, with typical understatement, in 1979.

The kingdom of Venkatagiri had stood for nearly a thousand years before it went the way of all the old Indian kingdoms with the coming of Independence in 1947—out of official existence. But the royal titles are still used unofficially by most of those who know the families.

Besides the Venkatagiri family, I have met other descendants of the old warrior caste at the Feet of Sai Baba. In Lord Sai they see the return of Lord Rama and Lord Krishna who stirred the world of their ancestors long ago.

• • •

Our next story, which concerns a great saint-composer, and a popular singer, is also associated with the House of Venkatagiri. The saint-composer Thyagaraja was born near Tanjore, in the south of Tamilnadu State (formerly Madras State) in the year 1757. He became a devotee of Lord Rama, practicing namasmarana to that Name with such constancy and fervor that, at age 30, he had a vision of Rama and his brother, Lakshmana.

Thyagaraja's love of Rama was expressed in his music. It is said that during his life he composed 4,000 songs to Lord Rama. Two hundred of these are still in use today, and many were made popular during the first half of the 20th century by the well-known singer Nagaratnama. She, herself, became a true devotee of Lord Rama.

When this greatly loved singer retired from the public stage, she went to live at the village, near Tanjore, where stood the tomb of Thyagaraja. In fact, it is said that she gave the bulk of the fortune she had made as a singer toward the improvement and upkeep of his *mahasamadhi* (holy tomb and place of worship).

During her retirement, Nagaratnama spent much time meditating on Lord Rama at the mahasamadhi of the great saint who had spent his life expressing his Rama devotion in the music she adored.

One day in the year 1951, while meditating on Rama by the saint's tomb, Nagaratnama had a vision. The form of Thyagaraja appeared before her and said: "Why seek Lord Rama here? He is now at Venkatagiri in the form of Sai Baba."

Nagaratnama, who had heard of Sai Baba, immediately sent a telegram to the Raja asking how long Sai Baba would be there, and if she could come to visit him. The Raja replied that the Lord would be there for some more days, and she was welcome to come to the palace.

The old singer set off that very day by car, and drove without resting the strenuous 400 miles or so to Venkatagiri. When, at the end of the long journey, Sai Baba stood before her, she saw the Form of Lord Rama, and went into a trance. She remained in the trance for several hours, until Baba put his hand on her head and brought her back to normal consciousness.

Then she had the ineffable joy of sitting beside Swami while together they sang Thyagaraja's songs of devotion. During the year following this blessed darshan of Lord Rama, the famous singer passed away.

Dattatreya

The next story I want to put on record here took place recently in the forest of the Bandipur Wild Life Sanctuary near the Nilgiri Hills. This is a favorite spot of the Lord who often passes that way on his journey to and from his house and school at Ootacamund (Ooty).

My wife and I were told about this event by two different people who had been witnesses. The first was Colonel Jogarao. Then a few days later, sitting in a car following Swami to Madras, we were told the same story by Mrs. Brij Ratanlal, who lives in a cottage at Brindavan near Swami. Like Martha of the Bible, her devotion is expressed by serving the Lord in many practical ways.

For instance, Mrs. Ratanlal is often permitted to travel with a group of devotees going somewhere with Swami. If there is to be an early start, and Swami plans to stop en route for a picnic meal, we have known her to spend most of the previous night cooking for the group picnic. Brij Ratanlal's food preparation is infused with love of the Lord and, like some other women devotees I know, she is therefore an excellent cook.

On this particular journey, she told us of many wonderful Sai experiences she had enjoyed, and we did not stop her when she came to the story we had already heard from Jogarao. We thought it would be a good thing to hear both versions. In fact, both versions were essentially the same. But each narrator supplied one or two details that the other had overlooked or perhaps did not even know. Here is the story compiled from both reports.

Colonel S. O. Jogarao (retired) of Indian Army Engineers is also a practical devotee. Most of his time is spent as a kind of chief executive for Baba's vast building program, and this, of course, brings him into frequent contact with the Lord for conferences and directions.

A happy, cheerful karma yogi, Jogarao cares nothing for the depths of metaphysics, but he had at this time a strong desire to see the "Divine Form." One day when he begged to be shown the "Divine Form" Swami smiled encouragingly, and Jogarao felt that soon he may be blessed with the vision.

Soon afterward Swami took him on a trip, along with a number of college students, Mrs. Ratanlal, and several other people. The party halted for a time in the forest of the Sanctuary, and soon one of the students began taking photographs with his Polaroid camera. Each photograph was a shot of Swami standing beside one of the people of the party, and as the photograph came out of the camera, Swami gave it to the person concerned. It was meant as a souvenir of the occasion.

Incidentally, I have sometimes been present when this kind of thing took place, and have a treasured souvenir of my wife and self standing beside Swami, the photograph having been taken during a luncheon halt in this same forest.

On this occasion, the two narrators told us, after many members of the party had been photographed with Swami, he said that he would be photographed alone, and stood well away from the group. As the student photographer began to focus the camera carefully, Mrs. Ratanlal came toward Swami and indicated that she would like to straighten his robe, so that the folds would fall nicely; she was like a mother who wants to arrange her child's clothes attractively before a photograph is taken.

"Stand back!" Swami ordered her in a loud, commanding voice. Alarmed, she jumped back, without touching his robe.

When the photograph came out of the camera, Swami told the student to give it to Jogarao. The latter, puzzled but pleased, stood holding the dark print while the image slowly came out. But instead of the well-known image of Satya Sai Baba, there appeared the form of Lord Dattatreya, with the three heads. Jogarao was stunned speechless; the Lord had anwered his prayer in a totally unexpected manner.

The photograph was passed around for everyone to see, and while they were looking at it, Swami said quietly to Mrs. Ratanlal, in explanation of his frightening command to her, "If you had touched me, the power would have killed you."

I understood this statement better after Gopal of Venkatagiri told me about an incident of Swami's early life. Once, Gopal said, when Swami was lying on a couch in one of the large rooms of the palace, he said to Gopal, "Don't grab my feet, but touch them lightly with the tips of your fingers."

Gopal did so and the power sent him reeling back across the room to bang against the opposite wall. It was like a high voltage electric shock, Gopal said.

Evidently the power going through Swami when he was creating the form of Dattatreya for the camera was strong enough to kill anyone who contacted it.

"I wonder why he showed you Dattatreya instead of Rama or Krishna, which seem to be the forms he takes most often?" I asked Jogarao.

"Oh, Dattatreya is his true form," Jogarao answered, shortly.

But a spiritual philosopher present remarked, "They are all his true forms; or rather, he has no true form at all."

That was the deepest truth, of course. Yet I felt that in Jogarao's remark there was some meaning, which he either could not explain or did not want to. Was there a special connection between the Dattatreya and the Sai forms?

Later some light was shed on this mystery when I read an article written by Dr. Charles White, then Professor of Philosophy and Religion at the American University, Washington, D.C.

Iris and I had known Charles White as a Theosophist and, at his request, had taken him to Sai Baba in 1970. He had brought with him one of his students who was an ordained Jesuit priest, studying comparative religion. Together they had made a film of Swami's activities to show to students in America.

The visit and the film were part of Dr. White's study of Hinduism through its past and present saints. Two years later he published in *The Journal of Asian Studies* (August, 1972) an article titled "The Sai Baba Movement: Approaches to the Study of Indian Saints." This was later brought out in booklet form, and Charles White kindly gave me a copy.

In the article he draws a line of connection between a number of saints, ascetics, and avatars. In the line are Goraknath (an ascetic of the 12th century), Kabir (poet-saint of the 15th century), Dattatreya (the sixth Avatar of Vishnu), Shirdi Sai Baba and Satya Sai Baba.

The main features White gives as common to these spiritual figures are: their attempts to unite different religions (particularly the Hindu and Moslem religions), their use of miraculous powers, the perpetual fire kept burning as the focus of religious life, and their extraordinary love of animals.

Taking the last feature first, iconographically Dattatreya is shown surrounded by animals, including dogs. Kabir and Shirdi Sai both had a great love of animals. Satya Sai has a veritable private zoo. With great love he cherishes many animals, including the elephant Sai Gita, a camel, many dogs, birds, rabbits, and spotted deer.

The perpetual fire feature continued with Shirdi Sai, but ended with Satya Sai. That is, it seems to have gone into another dimension from which it provides a ready supply of holy ash, which is called vibhuti.

The miraculous powers of the others are enhanced in Satya Sai, and he continues on a larger scale their attempts to unite different religions.

I discussed Dr. White's article with some of Baba's most erudite and devoted followers. Most of them seemed to think that there was something in White's ideas—some elusive link between our present Avatar, Dattatreya, Kabir, and possibly Goraknath. But none could explain what it was.

In his *Life of Sai Baba*, the biographer, H. H. Narasimha Swamiji, reports that Shirdi Sai Baba told his followers he had been Kabir in a former life. And there is no doubt that Satya Sai is a reincarnation of Shirdi Sai.[1]

---

[1] H. H. Narasimha Swamiji, *Life of Sai Baba* (Madras, India: All India Sai Samaj, 1955).

Moreover, Sri N. Kasturi records an event that appears to have some significance in this connection. Briefly, it is as follows: a worshiper of Dattatreya asked his old guru to go to Puttaparti for the blessings of Sri Satya Sai Baba who was, he said, an incarnation of Dattatreya. The guru replied that he was, himself, too old for the journey, but that his pupil should go there for Baba's darshan.

The Dattatreya disciple did so and was called for an interview. Swami's first words to him were: "Come on! Have your *namaskaram* (make your obeisance). This is the Dattatreya *Peetham* (base, site, resting place) for you."

Kasturi writes: "Dattatreya is extolled in the *Puranas* as 'He who goes to every place at the same instant' in answer to calls, prayers, supplications from all quarters for intercession and solace and strength and relief." These words could have been written to describe Sai Baba.[2]

So, though in essence all avatars are aware of their oneness with God, and identity with each other, at another level there may be special relationships. As persons there may be particular links and personality likenesses between certain saints and avatars. The one unique Divine Person could have incarnated at different periods as, for instance, Kabir, Dattatreya, and Sai Baba.

---

[2] N. Kasturi, *The Life of Bhagavan Sri Satya Sai Baba*, Vol. 1, p. 219.

CHAPTER SIX

Changing and Saving People

MANY PEOPLE HAVE said that Sai Baba's greatest miracle is the way he changes the hearts and minds and lives of human beings. The change is toward better health, greater happiness, and more meaningful, more enlightened living.

This is no easy matter because we have freedom of will, or at least, a good degree of it. Our greatest desire is to be free, for God has made us that way. But with freedom goes responsibility. And because the human mind makes many mistakes, the price of freedom must be suffering. Only through suffering from our errors will we gain the all-wisdom that makes no errors. The spiritual growth that leads to the all-wisdom must be gained in the school of adversity.

So, if it is part of God's contract not to manipulate us like puppets on strings, how can He change us? By what power can God alter the inner person, and so save humanity from the suicidal outcome of its own constant, cumulative mistakes? Not by wise and convincing arguments to the thinking mind, but only by the subtle, persuasive power of love will the alchemy of human transformation be brought about. Sometimes this is a speedy process but more often it is a slow one. We can see examples of both at work around Sai Baba.

No one observer can ever see more than a small cross-section of the thousands of individuals in whom Baba has wrought the inner change. But from the cross-section we can get some idea of the whole picture. The majority of people come first to Sai Baba with some worldly problem. He solves the problem and, at the same time, works a subtle change in the people, themselves. Years later they see that the problems were really small matters, but the change wrought in themselves was very great indeed.

I, myself, had no specific worldly problem for him to solve when I first came to Swami. I was the philosopher wandering the world in search of Truth with the small lamp of the mind.

In my search I had found a few nuggets of the truth that widens the mental horizon and brings pleasure and satisfaction to the mind. But there was still an inner dissatisfaction, a hunger for something more, for some inner secret that would bring fulfillment and peace to the whole being.

Then in the moment when I was first alone with Satya Sai Baba, his miraculous shaft of Divine Love penetrated the calcified shell of my heart, and a sea-change began. The impact was sudden and tremendous, but its outward results in my life were gradual. Let me try to describe some of these results.

I found myself standing, mentally, at a new lookout point from which the panorama of life was different. The light was shining less strongly on some old familiar peaks, while some others were coming into clearer, brighter focus. For instance, the peaks of material success, of fame, of worldly pleasures were fading into the background. They were still visible but becoming less enticing. Instead, other pinnacles began to call to the heart and ask to be scaled. Some of these might be called service to God, to mankind, to Divine Understanding.

I already knew that my dharma was to write. Swami confirmed this. But through his influence, without a word spoken on that subject, my motivation changed. Instead of writing primarily for name, fame, and fortune, or simply for making a living, as before, I set my sights on another target.

Henceforth, come what may, I would strive to express the Truth as I saw it, and in this way spend my days serving God and humanity.

I do not claim to have reached the high pinnacles of *nishkamakarma* (desireless action), but I try to do my duty with love, leaving the results of my actions entirely to God. I try. And so I have found a happier, more satisfying outlook on work.

But, quite apart from this basic change in work motivation, I have, through the benign influence of my Avatar-guru, developed a steadier, more understanding, more creative approach to life in general. I am fortunate that my wife and I found Swami together. Very soon after we came to him, he told us that our marriage was firmly based on a deep spiritual unity and an abiding friendship from an earlier life.

"There were just the two of you," was his pointed description of our relationship. Then he added enigmatically, "But now there are three of us."

At first we missed the profound truth in that simple statement, but later we understood fully what he had meant. Now we feel that he is always with us—the most important one of the three. The ingredient of Divine Love is written with increasing content into the prescription for each day. When fear or worry try to beset us, we remember his words, "Why fear when I am here?" So, as he is always here, why fear at all?

Life certainly gains a new meaning when you know, beyond doubt, that God is within and all around you, guiding your footsteps, understanding and forgiving when those footsteps falter. Swami has set the goal before us, and though the road must sometimes be difficult, we know the true purpose and object of life, and are assured that we will reach it in the end. Such sure knowledge brings a steady undertone of joy and peace that makes us realize how empty life was before we knew the love of the Lord.

Many Sai devotees with whom I have talked on such matters tell me how Baba has changed the quality of their lives by, likewise, giving them a new set of values—replacing the pleasures of the senses with more enduring, more fulfilling spiritual joys.

A good example is Dr. Prakash Sharma who had a prosperous medical practice in Australia. "I used to enjoy myself—or think I did—drinking alcohol, smoking cigarettes, and talking empty talk at cocktail parties and club gatherings," he said. In short, soon after he came to Australia, he joined heartily in the country's typical social life.

Being a newcomer, he did not know the wiles of certain unscrupulous builders, exploiting a housing boom in the state. Getting into the clutches of one of these, through social contacts, he lost thousands of dollars and met with tremendous difficulties in getting a house built for himself and his family. At the same time, through slanderous tongues, his medical practice fell away to almost nothing.

At about this time, the doctor came into contact with some members of the Sai Family in Sydney and began attending meetings at a Sai Centre. Then he started to feel that Swami was with him, helping him in all his difficult problems. In fact, his faith grew stronger as adversity intensified, and in the end he came out on top. Truly on top, because he has completely forgiven those who wronged him. "It was through them," he said, "and the suffering they brought, that I came closer and closer to Swami. So, really, I should thank them for what they did."

The transformation that enabled him to forgive his enemies brought also a complete change in his social tastes and habits. "Now I have Swami, I don't want the social activities I used to indulge in. I just like being at home with my family, or meeting Sai friends and talking about the Lord. I am very much happier, too."

Dr. Sharma started bhajan and study meetings in his new home as soon as it was completed. Then came a strong desire to serve the Lord by doing some free medical work wherever it was most required. In the end he decided that the greatest need for this was back in his own country. So, with the full agreement of his wife and two children, all keen Sai devotees, he gave up his again prosperous practice, sold his house and all his goods, and returned to India.

He knew quite well that the material standards of comfort for himself and family would drop considerably. "But never mind that," he said, "I will be serving the Lord better by helping my own people." He also hoped that his children, a boy and a girl, would find places in Swami's colleges – and so have the best possible education.

Changing "Dogs" to "Lamps"

At this stage Swami is concentrating on the education of youth, and this is where the deep changes he brings to human character are seen most strikingly.

A great educationist of India stated recently that the violent patterns of behavior (so widespread in the universities of the West) have come to India. Drug addiction, licentious living, alcoholism, political agitation, with threats of violence, are part of the pattern. Indian parents are very reluctant to send their children into this corrupting and demoralizing atmosphere. But what alternative do they have?

Even a brief association with the Sri Satya Sai Colleges is enough to show that the student life in them is in complete contrast to the ugly, depressing patterns that are becoming common elsewhere.

Dr. S. Bhagavantham, who is a close and keen observer of the Sai Colleges, paints the picture much better than I could. In an article in the *Golden Age* he writes:

> One has only to see how any one of the Satya Sai Colleges is run, and to visit one of the college hostels, even as a casual guest, to see what the inmates are like, and to know what the practised ideals and ways of living are.

. . . In these colleges dignity of labour and simple living are not merely talked of, but practised. . . . Students work in the kitchen, in the dairy, in the hospital and in the villages. It has been said that there is not a skill nor a branch of learning in which the students of these colleges do not acquire a high degree of proficiency. . . . Amongst them one can find dancers, singers, cooks, servers and nurses; public speakers, orators, electricians, radio mechanics and *Vedic* pundits exhibiting their skills in an expert manner, but with commendable humility. Readiness to serve the needy and the sick in a selfless manner is so obvious amongst the students that persons who are put into the hostels to live temporarily with the students often feel ashamed of the pride and ego they bring with them.

What is not easily explainable is that amidst all the other activities, academic excellence stands out, and is demonstrated each year by the several high ranks which the students of these colleges secure in all the examinations conducted by the respective universities.

One noteworthy feature is the fact that there are quite a few students who are, as it were, the spoilt children of affluent parents, educated in other schools until they are completely corrupted, and given up by their parents as irretrievable. Such youngsters, after joining the Satya Sai Colleges and hostels, so change that their parents and former teachers cannot believe their own eyes when they see the changed products. One only has to speak to such parents, as I have often done, to realise how grateful they are to Providence for having brought their children into a unique educational institution, providing a new way of life for youth. This transformation of young people is the biggest miracle, and the most astonishing one, amongst all the miracles I have seen Sri Satya Sai

Baba perform. Each delinquent is handled in a way that suits his case, and no two are alike.[1]

"He changes us from street dogs to street lamps," wrote one student succinctly. Adding my own testimony to that of the worthy doctor, I have been amazed and enthralled to see the way in which these students serve their elders, with alacrity and sincere respect, whenever the opportunity arises. All of them are quiet, speak only when necessary, and their manners are perfect. It is a joy to be with such young sons of God, and to address them in their lecture rooms, as I have had the honor of doing on several occasions.

Once, for instance, when I had just arrived back in India, I went, unsuspectingly, into an assembly of students and teachers to hear Swami speak. But before he began, he called me forward and said, "Give these students some advice! About ten minutes."

I was taken unawares. How was I to give advice to these young men who seemed well nigh perfect? But when Swami says, "Speak," one speaks. The theme of my short address was their good fortune in being in such an institution of learning, under the direct influence of the Avatar. My advice was that they should prepare themselves to be what I was sure they had been chosen to be—the perfect instuments for use in the Avatar's divine mission. Wherever they found themselves after student days, they should always remember their role as God's helpers for the salvation of humanity.

Swami then stood up and spent about an hour giving them a verbal thrashing. I was amazed. But, sitting out in front of them, I was able to watch the sea of eager young faces. Strangely, they seemed not at all downcast by the stern censure they were getting from Swami. Their faces continued to glow with love and veneration as they drank in every word.

---

[1] From an article by Dr. S. Bhagavantham in *Golden Age*, 1979, an annual ashram magazine published by Prasanthi Nilayam Press, India.

I began to think that perhaps I was wrong in praising them when Swami was doing just the opposite. But afterward, as he went out, he looked at me, smiled and said, "That was good advice you gave them."

Then I spoke to the College Principal, our old friend, Professor D. Narender. Why, I asked him, was Swami chastising the students in that way?

"Oh," he replied, "one or two of them have been misbehaving themselves. Those whom the cap fits, wear it. The others get a healthy reminder of the high standards required."

"But they looked so unperturbed — quite happy, in fact!"

"Well, they are always happy to be at Swami's feet, and hear him speak, whatever he might be saying. They know he loves them," Narender explained.

That is the key. Swami is a strict disciplinarian, but his great love heals any wounds that might be inflicted by sharp verbal caning.

Crocodile Jaws

I have heard of cases where the Divine Grace of Lord Sai has rescued people from the jaws of destruction through addiction to drugs. I know personally of several.

There was, for instance, the young woman from a European country who, for obvious reasons, shall be nameless. My wife and I came to know her well on one of our sojourns at Swami's ashrams.

She had been on heroin for many years when she first came to Sai Baba, hoping desperately for help. Amazingly, from the moment she saw him, her compelling desire for the drug seemed to vanish. He told her to stay in India near him because, if she returned to her own country, she would soon be dead. She knew that he meant she would be unable, then, to resist the bad influence of her old drug associates.

Staying near Swami was an easy therapy for her. If she had any of the usual drug withdrawal symptoms, she never mentioned them. And no difficulties or discomforts seemed to trouble her. If Swami went from Whitefield to Puttaparti, or vice versa, she would jump on some primitive bus, and be at the new destination soon after he was. Rigors of public transport, austerities of accommodation, Indian food problems, the heat of the Indian summer, language difficulties, misunderstandings with local people; instead of such difficulties and upsets drawing her back to the drug escape, as might be expected, they were all as nothing—washed away in the constant flow of the Lord's Love.

When we last saw her she had been with Swami for many months. He was the center of her life—her rehabilitation center *par excellence*—saving her from destruction and leading her back to a normal life. The time would come when she could return safely to her own country.

The next case has a particular interest because it concerns a medical doctor in the district of Sai Baba's birthplace. The doctor was, he states, at high school with Satyanarayana Raju (Satya Sai Baba). He wrote the story for the *Sanathana Sarathi* (the ashram magazine) a few years ago, and here it is, essentially as he told it.

"I am a registered medical practitioner, engaged for some years in my profession at Uravakonda, Anantapur District, Andhra Pradesh. As a result of some unforeseen circumstances and their effect on my mental condition, I got involved in the vicious habit of taking injections of morphia.

"It began with two injections a day. Within eight days, that is, from the 20th of June, 1968, I was taking four injections a day. In another fortnight I needed eight, and within a month after that I was forced to give myself sixteen injections per day. A month later the quantity my body clamoured for increased to twenty injections. This continued for three months, then I had to take thirty injections everyday. I could not find any way to reduce the intake.

"My income from medical practice was about 800–1000 rupees per month. That proved insufficient for the morphia I had to give myself. So I sold five acres of my land for 13,000 rupees. This, added to my income, sufficed for only sixteen months.

Then I sold three acres for 10,000 rupees and that somehow got me through another sixteen months of slavery to the habit.

"At the end of that period I had no money remaining, so I sold the building sites I owned in the town for 6,000 rupees, and spent it on the morphia during the next eight months.

"I have ten children — six girls and four boys. My wife had died. I had not been giving any consideration to how the poor children were managing to exist. They obviously suffered for want of food and clothing, and went through manifold miseries. They used to wait outside my room and when they saw some patient giving me money, they would cry piteously, 'Father! Give it to us. We'll buy some grain with it, some snacks!' But I used to drive them away with foul interjections. I was not concerned about what they ate or how they managed.

"Evidently, some patients used to give the children, now and then, part of any fees owing to me, and from this meagre source they kept flesh and bone together. Nine years passed thus.

"I was in a state of deep despair. I could not reduce the intake in the slightest. When I was forced on some days to take less than usual, I suffered extreme agony: pain all over the body, yawning, sweating, fear, effusion of saliva, stuttering, cramps — all these gave me great distress.

"On account of the high cost of the habit my family had been ruined, my medical practice declined and almost dried up, and my physical health deteriorated from day to day. How could I escape from the coils of the drug? What could I do?

"One of my friends who had fallen victim to morphia had gone to Madras for a cranial operation by which they said the habit would be cured. Another doctor friend, too, had gone to Madras and stayed for a treatment taking three or four months. He was cured of the morphia habit, but it had cost the first friend 3,500 rupees, and the second, 5,000 rupees. Though I wanted to go, too, I did not have the money for it.

"To continue the injections I begged, borrowed, visited hospitals and somehow managed to get sufficient morphia for my minimum daily quota of thirty to thirty-five injections. In the nine years I had run through 40,000 rupees, yet I could not escape the habit, nor even reduce the intake. One can free oneself from the jaws of a crocodile sooner than from the jaws of morphia.

"Meanwhile the devotees of Bhagavan Sri Satya Sai Baba had begun a *bhajan samaj* in our town. It was organised by my friend, Dr. N. Anjaneyulu, M.A., Ph.D., and was held every Thursday at the Subrahmaneswara Temple near my house. One Thursday I went into the temple and sat in a distant corner listening to the *bhajan* songs.

"During the singing a thought arose in my mind: 'Baba! You were my classmate here in the High School, years ago. You must be remembering me. You must be knowing the depths to which this habit has dragged me. There are some who doubt you, and many who adore you as God. I am not involving myself in that controversy now. I want to find, from my own experience, the Truth. Well, if you can bless me with the mental courage and strength to get out of this vicious morphia habit, I shall believe that you are God.' With this vow, taken with a full heart, I steadied myself.

"Within a few seconds the *bhajan* ended. They distributed *vibhuti prasad* to everyone. Holding the packets in my palm as a precious gift, and resolving to rely upon Baba for the strength to free myself, I returned home.

"I decided that, whatever might happen, however hard the conditions, I would not take a single injection of morphia for a full three days. 'If on the fourth day I am free from the tentacles of morphia, I shall adore Baba just as those people are doing at the temple,' I told myself.

"On the first day I did not take any injection – not even one. I had no calls of nature that day. I had profuse sweating, cramps in muscles, a burning sensation all over the body, wild imaginings, streams of tears and a cough. These gave me a terrible time. But I swallowed small quantities of *vibhuti* and carried on.

"The second day was worse. The urine and faeces were full of blood; frightful thoughts of suicide haunted me. When the third day dawned I thought that I may not even survive it. By night time I was shouting and wailing aloud. I hit the floor with my feet. I hit my head against a pillar. I blabbered wildly and loudly. The children wept and wailed, awakening the neighbours. Some friends came in and, seeing my condition, shed tears in sympathy with the children.

"During the night a doctor friend came in, and understanding the reason for my pitiable condition, he brought four injections of morphia, and advised that I take some.

"I replied, 'Doctor, the promise I have given to Swami will lapse tomorrow. Keep the injections safe until morning.'

"The time was then 3:45 A.M. My children were sitting around me. I said to my little daughter, Hafiza Begum, 'Go and get me the *vibhuti* of Swami I have kept on that shelf over there.' She brought it. I took a pinch, placed it on my tongue and drank some water to wash it down.

"In about ten minutes I fell asleep. During the sleep I felt as if I was on a pilgrimage, and did not wake until 11 A.M. the next day. That was the fourth day. As promised, the doctor friend, hearing that I was awake, came with the morphia injections.

" 'Dear friend. how do you feel?' he asked, softly.

"I replied, equally softly, 'By Swami's grace my mind is clear and calm.'

" 'In that case I believe you have no need of this morphia.'

"In a firm tone I replied, 'No, there is no need.'

"The doctor was overjoyed. 'Ah! What happy news you have given us. How pleasant to the ears. Swami has showered his grace on you,' he said. Going out to the fruit shop, he bought two apples for me and, placing them in my hands, he left, taking the morphia with him.

"Since that day, three months back, I have never had the slightest inclination towards morphia. My health is getting better and better everyday. My medical practice has picked up, and my children are happy.

"On the Wednesday after my escape from the hold of the crocodile, I joined the *nagarasankirtan* group that passed my house and, reaching the Subrahmanyeswara Temple with them, I related to all the devotees of Bhagavan the story of my vow and its fulfillment.

"My friends, relatives and well-wishers were all very happy when they came to know of Baba's grace. I have now no doubt that the Divine Will of Swami can cure everyone suffering from such vicious habits, provided they surrender to him. For myself, I am convinced that he is Divine and that His Grace alone has saved me."

• • •

The doctor, whose name is K. Meera Mohiaddin, wrote the above account of his experience three months after his cure, that is, in 1977. Three years later, in 1980, I wrote asking his permission to include it in this book. He readily gave the permission, saying, "I am immensely happy to note that my experience of Bhagavan's grace will be of some use to you in writing your third book."

I, myself, was happy, but not at all surprised, to find that he was still living a normal, healthy life, well clear of the "crocodile's jaws," and that he was still an ardent devotee of Sai Baba, looking forward to attending Swami's third World Conference at Prasanti Nilayam in November of that year.

CHAPTER SEVEN

Sai Teachings and the Sai Path

MANY BOOKS HAVE been written and no doubt many more will be written on the Sai teachings and the Sai path. But it is a busy world and most people are not inclined to plough through numerous volumes on a subject. Not, at least, until they come to see its vital concern in their lives. So I will try to give the essentials of the Sai teachings and guidance in this chapter.

What does he say about those great questions that come to mind when we pause to think about the ultimate meaning of things—God, Man, the Universe, the purpose of life, and how we should live to find true happiness?

God

"God is everywhere and in everything. The whole creation is from Him and He is in the creation," says Baba. So we can think of God as the formless Essence of all existence, or as the basic Force behind all the forces, or energies, that go to make up the universe. All things have a beginning and an ending, except this one divine Essence or Force. Like the circumference of a circle, it has no beginning and no ending. It is eternal.

This formless God sounds more like a Principle than a Person. A person has limitations while God has none. Yet a principle has no life, while God is all Life. Baba says: "God is not 'It'; to say 'It' would be to lead one to think of inert matter." In reality God is beyond the categories of human thought, being neither It, nor He, nor She.

We must use some pronoun in speaking of God. Generally we use the pronoun "He," but we should remember that this divine "He" is beyond the limitations of personality. Furthermore, we must also understand that the fundamental, formless God can and does take Form, putting part of His infinite Self into finite Form. In fact, Baba teaches the Vedantic doctrine that God has taken all the forms around us, including the one you see when you look in a mirror.

We could find God in any form, provided we see the divine Essence within the form. Indeed, God has been worshipped in thousands of forms—human and otherwise—since the world began. But, though the forms are many, there is only the One God. Swami uses the analogy of electricity to illustrate this; when you turn on the switch, the electric globe is lighted. But it is the same electricity that lights up all the globes. The globes that shine brightest with the Divine Electricity are the ones we worship as Gods of Form.

When an author creates a story or drama, he puts part of himself in all the characters—perhaps more into some than others. Yet while existing within his characters, there is much more of himself beyond them. In the same way God exists infinitely beyond His creation. Within the forest, the flower, the bird, the beast, and humans, He is the immanent God. Beyond it all He is the transcendent God.

He is nearer to you than your own breathing, while at the same time far off in the infinite. We can never see Him or understand Him. But we can experience Him.

Human Beings

"Who are you?" Baba often asks people. They know he does not refer to their names, so they flounder, not knowing really who they are.

The first thing he instills into us is that we are not our bodies. The body is part of the ever-changing universe. In fact, it is, itself, a mini-universe, a replica of the greater one—and, therefore, a mystery.

Just as God is within and beyond His great universe, so the true human being is within and beyond this mini-universe. This true human may be called the spirit or the soul or, as Swami calls it, the atma.

This spirit of man (or each human being) was not created when the rest of the universe was created. It has existed and will exist throughout eternity. In some inexplicable, mysterious way the true man is one with God and is co-eternal with Him.

The simple answer to Swami's question, therefore, is: "I am the *atma*, or the divine spirit." He will be equally satisfied if you reply: "I am I," for that means the same thing.

The fact that we are, in essence, one with God is, perhaps, the salient point of Baba's teachings. At least he seems to emphasize it more than anything else. It is not, of course, a new concept. We find it in the ancient Upanishads, and it has been stated by all the great spiritual teachers. Stated by them briefly, in passing, so to speak, but not emphasized. Now it is really being emphasized, as if the Divine Mind knows that the time is ripe to come to grips with this mighty Truth. Perhaps now we can at last receive it.

But if we humans have all come from God, from the One God, as Swami teaches, why have we forgotten, why are we so completely unaware of our true identity? It is as if a cloud of ignorance falls over our minds when we are born. In early childhood we have brief glimpses of glory through the cloud—intimations of immortality, as the poet calls it. But as the years pass, we become more enmeshed in the world's sensual allurements and attachments. Forgetting our true identity completely, we embrace a new one, built on our animal instincts, desires, and worldly ambitions. This is the lower, troublesome ego.

The reason why we are here in the schoolroom of earth is surely that we may learn some valuable lessons, and develop strong, noble characters—as Swami teaches. But why must we entirely forget who we are in order to do this? Many speculative theories have been put forward concerning this deep question. The real answer is, I think, known only to God—and He keeps the secret. It remains a mystery for solution in Eternity.

The lessons we have to learn, the development of character we must attain, our final awakening to our true Selves, are things that take many lifetimes. Hence the doctrine of reincarnation, taught by Sai Baba, in concordance with the spiritual philosophy of Hinduism and Buddhism.

The Universe

The universe of multitudinous forms, from invisible microscopic life to the invisible far distant stars, had a beginning, so it will, of course, have an end. It was created by the eternal God, not out of nothing, but out of His infinite Self. The One created the appearance of the ever-changing many, while still remaining the One.

The universe, appearing as many things, is, therefore, called the "Becoming" mode of God. The One, behind the dynamic appearance, is known as the "Being" mode. If we could see the Being mode, the changeless Divine, within and beyond the constantly Becoming mode, we would see truly.

But normally we do not see this God-in-the-universe. Moreover, we do not even see the changing mode as it really is. As the sages of all times and climes—including Socrates—have said, our senses and minds play us false. They build a picture of solid, many-colored, three-dimensional objects, whereas—as science now agrees—what is really playing on our senses is a web of energy patterns, moving at super-high speeds in vast empty spaces.

So what we think we see is *maya*—it is not really there. And what is really there is forever changing anyway—except for the constant changeless One behind it all. Swami likens it to a moving picture show. Flickering patterns of light and shade throw the illusion of moving forms on the still, unchanging screen.

When the reel of film ends, the forms vanish, but the screen remains. It represents the "Being" mode of God.

But another show will soon begin. Another Cosmic Drama will be projected onto the screen of the "Being" God. Phenomenal universes come and go periodically. We ourselves are part of this dynamic Cosmic Drama. At least our bodies and minds are. But within each one of us is the unchanging Divine Being. And that is the true Self.

The Purpose of Life

In times of difficulty or tragedy, if not at other times, people ask themselves the question: what is the purpose of life? For most of their days they have acted as if the purpose of existence is to make a lot of money, rise to a position of importance, become famous or powerful, or perhaps just to enjoy themselves, wallowing in the world of sensual desire. They think that the achievement of such goals will bring them happiness.

But then one day when, maybe, for one reason or another, they must look death squarely in the face, and realize how close it always stands, they begin to doubt the validity of such goals. But what is the true goal, they wonder? What will bring the abiding state of happiness for which the human heart forever yearns? Can it only be found in some wish-fulfilling heaven in the skies?

Sai Baba teaches that the purpose of life is to find out who we really are. The human being, he says, is like the prince who was stolen by robbers when he was a baby. He has grown up to think that he is one of the robbers. But if he finds out, and comes to know beyond doubt, that he is a prince with a wonderful inheritance, his life and outlook will be completely changed.

Likewise, if we can reach direct, doubt-free knowledge of our true identity, then our lives will move onto a new level, and our outlook will change completely. Accompanying that change will be an abiding joy that is unaffected by the ups and downs of circumstance. Discovering who we are releases this joy, which is a part of our true nature.

We do not have to wait until we die, and move to some other zone of existence, before making the great discovery. In fact it is better that we make it here—and that is the purpose of our human lives on earth.

When we have found the real hidden Self, we have found God, for He is one with that Self. The inward journey to the Self and to God may have three stages. First, there is the feeling that God is the Master, a great Being out there somewhere, and that we are His servants. Then seekers come closer and understand that each of them is the son, the offspring, of God; finally they realize they are one with God.

When seekers realize that they are one with God, they will know also that they are one with all life, for God is all life. While they continue to live in the world, thereafter, life will be governed by this sense of harmonious unity. They will not seek happiness and satisfaction through the things of the world. Happiness will be always with them. They will seek only to serve their fellow human beings in order to bring all people to the goal that they have, themselves, reached.

How to Achieve the Purpose

There is no Aladdin's lamp that we can rub to bring the treasure suddenly before us. Nor do we have to travel the world to find the treasure, like the man who sought it in every country, then returned home to find it hidden under the floor of his humble cottage.

Every great teacher who has given directions for reaching the goal of life has given what might be called a formula. But it is never a magical formula that can be mixed and stirred to give immediate results. It is always a formula by which we must strive to live our lives. When we can manage to do so, the results are certain.

As might be expected, the formulae are basically the same if we can analyze them correctly—as we shall see in later chapters. The only differences are in the ways they are set out, in the emphasis given to one factor or another, or in the introduction of a new ingredient to suit the spirit of an age or the widening thoughts of people who search.

Sai Baba has given us a formula with four main ingredients. Perhaps instead of thinking of them as ingredients we should regard them as four guidelines along the Sai Path. If we follow these guidelines, we shall surely reach the goal. Their Sanskrit names are *Prema*, *Satya*, *Dharma* and *Shanti*. I shall try to explain what is implied by each in Baba's teachings.

Prema

Prema is Divine Love, the love that by its nature gives continuously, asking nothing in return. It is the love that God has for all creatures. We each can develop that love, for we have it inherently as part of our inner divine nature. But the way must be opened so that this love, trapped in the spiritual heart, can flow outward.

From the spring in the heart, the stream of love flows toward the great ocean of love which is God. Because God is within all people, Divine Love from the individual heart flows toward all. It has, says Swami, "the quality of sympathy, sympathy which makes one happy when others are happy and miserable when others are unhappy." It shows itself as "a series of little acts, directed by the attitude of reverence for the divinity of all beings."

I know from experience that Swami, himself, being the great body-of-love, opens the way to release the spring in the spiritual heart. There is such a powerful aura of love around him that, like a flame, it burns away the debris that is holding back the stream of prema from our true nature. Then the wonderful stream begins to flow—toward God and toward all life.

It can be blocked again by the heavy sediment of selfishness, egotism, wrong thinking, and all the slush that comes from the boglands of desire. Baba gives many instructions on how to live in this world and still keep the pure stream of prema flowing. Here are a few of them.

"Consider always the faults of others, however big, to be insignificant and negligible, and consider your own faults, however insignificant and negligible, to be big—and feel repentant."

"Realize that the one and only God resides in the heart of all creatures, and try to love them all. Try to understand the fatherhood of God and the brotherhood of all creatures. Realize that God is pure love, that He is *Prema-swarupa* (the embodiment of love)."

We should put this brotherhood toward all creatures into practice, he says, by remembering every day to "start the day with love, fill the day with love, and end the day with love. That is the way to God, for God is Love."

What a difference it will make to our days if we remember this maxim each morning when we awake, and recall it from time to time as the events of the day march by!

But why then are we equipped with critical faculties if we must refrain from criticizing and judging other people? Swami teaches that we should criticize the actions of a person rather than the person himself. In fact, we must guard diligently against judging others, and talking about their faults and weaknesses.

For one thing, we cannot see deeply into the heart of our brother. To illustrate this, Swami tells the story of a married couple who were walking through a forest to a place of pilgrimage. The husband, who was walking in front, saw a diamond glittering in the sand of the path. Quickly he kicked some sand over the stone so that his wife would not see it. He was afraid that she would pick it up and become enslaved by the tinsel—which was how he regarded the diamond.

But the wife had seen the jewel and the gesture. She chided her husband for feeling in his mind any distinction between the diamond and the sand. For her, she said, they were just the same. So the husband had certainly failed to see into the heart of his wife.

When our spiritual perception is sufficiently developed to see deeply into the human soul, our feeling of unity with all will be such that any criticisms we must make will be cushioned in kindly understanding and love. Swami, himself, exemplifies this. His criticisms, given with love and divine understanding, are the only kind from which anyone will ever learn. All else are egos barking, unavailingly, at one another like noisy dogs.

As we move along the path by the prema guideline, our attachment to worldly things will, one by one, dissolve away. At the same time our attachment to God will strengthen, so that we become ever aware of His presence. We begin to understand, too, the occult law that by seeking the kingdom of God, all the things that we need in the world come to us.

Swami puts it simply: "If we have complete faith, and surrender completely to God, then, as the cat takes care of its kittens, God Himself will look after our welfare wherever we are."

But even when we see that it is the right thing to unite our will to the Divine Will—which is what surrender means—how do we learn to know God's will? How can we divine it in all situations?

The block that prevents us perceiving God's will is our own egotism. This is something, Baba says, "that has been inherring in man for ages, sending its tentacles deeper and deeper with the experience of every succeeding life." Devotion to God, he says, is the water with which to wash away this dirt of the ages. To this water of devotion we should, however, add the twin detergents of discrimination and non-attachment—discrimination between the false and the true, and breaking our attachment to the false. The soap of sadhana (spiritual practices) must also be used in washing away the last dregs of egotism.

The ego, the false "I," dies a slow and painful death on the cross of sadhana. But die it will, and then comes the resurrection of the real "I."

As the earliest Sufi poet of Persia, Baba Kuhi, put it, "I passed away, into nothingness, I vanished, and lo, I was the All-living—only God I saw."[1]

On the Sai Path, the guideline of prema is the most important. It leads to a growing devotion to God, and is sustained by the bliss that comes from that devotion. Seekers help each other by gathering together to sing and talk of the glories of God, or the particular form of God they worship. They should avoid controversy because this leads to egotism and the love of conquest. As there is room for a diversity of views, controversiality can never lead to a final conclusion. Rather than waste time in debate, the seeker should use every minute in promoting devotion to God.

"Supreme love and supreme wisdom are one," said the great sage Narada. "Sing then the glories of the Lord that he may abide in the hearts of all . . . bringing them everlasting peace."[2]

But although the pinnacle of love is wisdom, until that high level is reached, seekers on the devotional path may become too emotional. Then, Swami points out, the devotion can blow away like thistle down. There must be an anchor of increasing knowledge or else the devotion will be lost in the void. And so he gives us the guideline of *Satya*.

Satya

This word comes from the Sanskrit *sat*, meaning "True Being," and satya is the guideline given by Satya Sai Baba to guide us in the search for the Truth of Being through the acquisition of knowledge.

There are two kinds of knowledge—secular and sacred. Both of these are taught in the institutions of learning established by Sai Baba. "If we do not gather information, it is not possible to

---

[1] Bābā Kūhī of Shīrāz. Part of a poem quoted in Reynold A. Nicholson's *The Mystics of Islam* (London: G. Bell & Sons, 1914), p. 59.

[2] Narada, *Narada's Bhakti Sutras* (Madras, India: Sri Ramakrishna Math Press, 1972).

achieve transformation," he says. The transformation his educational programs aim to achieve is primarily one of character. Both types of knowledge are used to this end.

In his writings and discourses, many of which have been published in book form, Baba concentrates on sacred knowledge—the mental understanding, so far as it can be given in words, of God, the Universe and our purpose here on Earth. The essence of his teachings on these themes was given briefly earlier in this chapter, but in his talks he gives many variations on these eternal themes.

There is need for such variations, different verbal approaches, emphasis, and illustration because of the differing mental and spiritual levels, and varied cultural backgrounds of his listeners. Thus he provides food for all of them.

Perhaps to average people who have cut their teeth on some orthodox religion, or no religion at all, Swami's teachings may at first sound rather strange, or even revolutionary—particularly the concept of our being one with God. But if we search through our own scriptures, we will find the same truth stated there, as it is in the writings of mystics.

To the student of the Ancient Wisdom, found at the base of all religions, Swami's verbal teachings ring no strange bell. They simply give new life and vitality to the spiritual verities that are as old as time. But the dust of ages has collected on the eternal bell of truth; it needs to be cleaned and polished so that it can again ring the Divine Message across the world. Baba is busy doing this.

Nevertheless, at the same time, Baba teaches that knowledge gained through the head can never, itself, take us to the goal of life. Indeed, the core of Satya lies deep in the spiritual heart. And it is from there that the most profound promptings and root ideas come. Yet they need to be channeled through the mind to be formulated into thoughts and words. To express the deepest heart-truths in words is, however, a difficult operation and perhaps never fully achieved. Hence the need of mythology to suggest such inexpressible truths.

Some people—by their temperaments and training—must begin the search for ultimate truth through knowledge, that is, along the Jnana pathway. All will find, however, that at some point they must meet and merge with the path of love and devotion. Knowledge alone will dry the heart and lead to egotism and spiritual pride. So it is most important to mix it, as soon as possible, with the lubricant of Divine Love.

Adi Shankara, who, on the pathway of Jnana, reached the pinnacle of glory and honor as an illustrious sage, finally said: "The divine name of Lord Hari and that alone is my support and refuge; there is no other effective path for attaining salvation in *Kali Yuga* (our present age)." In order to foster love of God in the hearts of men, Adi Shankara composed and gave to the world many devotional hymns, including the well known "Bhaja Govindam."

While putting devotion uppermost, Sai Baba strives to balance this with knowledge. Satya Sai groups around the world meet to sing devotional songs (bhajans). This practice they enjoy above all things, and many would like to do nothing else at the meetings. But Swami insists that they incorporate regular periods of study and discussion to increase their knowledge and understanding, and lead to a balanced development.

The Sai Path integrates heart, head, and also hand. So another guideline is *Dharma*.

Dharma

From the Sanskrit verb root *dhri* (to hold), *dharma* is that which holds together our inner and outer activities. A simple definition of Dharma is Prema and Satya in action.

When Divine Love directs our footsteps, and the way is illumined by Divine Wisdom, all we do will be true to the highest dharma. But until that time is reached, we must avoid acting according to the whims of the desire-mind and calling that our dharma.

What then is to be our guide? Signposts for the direction of our actions are set out in the scriptures of the great religions. So the scriptures are one guide to right dharma in its aspect of righteousness, morality, goodness and justice.

Today we have, also, for guidance, the interpretative teachings of Swami. He has renewed and repainted the old signposts. But if we still find it hard sometimes to make the right decisions, Baba's grace is always there to help us.

There is, moreover, the formula of Karma Yoga which Swami often mentions as the ideal to keep before us in all we do. "Do not hunger after the fruits of your actions. Do your duty with Love in your heart and leave the results of all your actions in the hands of God."

This is an ideal to be reached progressively. When we work primarily for the welfare of our families, it is a beginning. When we have included the welfare of mankind, we have come near the ideal. It is reached when we can discern the Divine Intent in all things, and work in harmony with that. This, of course, requires great love and great wisdom, but we must keep moving toward it.

Here are some pointers that Baba has given to prevent our footsteps from going astray.

"Whoever subdues egotism, conquers selfish desires, destroys bestial feelings and impulses, and gives up the natural tendency to regard the body as the self, is surely on the path of *Dharma*."

"In all your worldly activities you should be careful not to wound propriety or the canons of good nature. You should not play false to the promptings of the Inner Voice, that is, you should at all times be prepared to respect the dictates of your conscience. You should watch your steps to see whether you are in someone's way. You should be ever vigilant to discover the Truth behind the scintillating variety of this world."

But, "The objective codes of *Dharma* relating to worldly activities and daily life, though important in their own sphere, have to be followed with the full knowledge and consciousness of the Inner Basic *Atmadharma* (the *Dharma* of the Divine Inner Self). Then only can the internal and external urges co-operate and yield the bliss of harmonious progress."

Because it is our basic purpose to find our way back to God, and that purpose must eventually be achieved, Dharma is "a flame of light that can never be extinguished." Yet though the flame cannot be extinguished, it may sometimes be eclipsed, as it is in the affairs of the world today.

Swami says, "When Dharma is not used to transmute human life, the world is afflicted by agony and fear; it becomes tormented by stormy revolutions."

In fact, "For a long time the spotless countenance of Dharma has been tarnished beyond recognition just as beautiful fields, through neglect, become unrecognisable thorny jungles. With the passage of time people become accustomed to the state of things around them, and do not notice the decline. This has happened to Dharma."

But the thorny jungle of the world's dharma must be cleaned up, and brought back to the smiling fields that it should be. This can be done by the Avatar and his helpers. All who love the good and the true must help in the restoration of the fair dharmic fields by, at least, giving up hatred toward others, and striving to cultivate tolerance, concord and amity.

"Through concord and amity the world will grow day by day into a place of happiness—free from disquiet, indiscipline, disorder and injustice."

Three Sai maxims for helping the individual live the dharmic life, and thus restore the fallen dharma of the world are:

"Do good; see good; be good. God loves the good."

"Duty, with love, is desirable. Love, without duty, is divine."

"Where Dharma is, God is; and where God is, there is victory."

Shanti

This is the unclouded inner peace that continues unabated, like Divine Bliss, whatever the ups and downs, the "glooms and gleams" of personal circumstances and the affairs of this world.

Swami says, "This *shanti* is the inner nature." So gaining the Peace is not a matter of acquiring something from outside, but of uncovering something already there. All sadhana helps in the

uncovering process. An important exercise in the spiritual discipline is the practice of discrimination. The aspirant should consciously discriminate between the false and the true, the tempo-
rary and the eternal, the unimportant and the vitally important.
Getting these priorities straight, he or she should be concerned
more with the important, true, eternal realities.

To our everyday, ordinary consciousness the things we desire seem naturally the most important. But if we use discrimination, as outlined above, and at the same time inquire deeply into
our hearts and minds, we will find that our worldly desires are
enemies of peace. They are clouds obscuring the bright skies of
that "peace that passeth understanding."

The constant struggle to obtain the desired objects brings
fear, frustration, dejection, anger, hatred. The competition with
others in the struggle also brings envy, jealousy, and other negative emotions. There can be no true peace while the mind is a
playground for such emotions.

What then can we do? Desire is an essential part of our animal nature. Down through the aeons of evolution, animal life
has used it, and the emotional responses it arouses, in order that
the individual and the species may survive. It is part of life's sur-
vival equipment.

Instinctive desires arise in the mind as in other animals. The
emotions, concomitant with the desires, are also felt in the
mind, but find expression in the body. From the constant play
of strong negative emotions, such as hatred, fear, anger and the
rest, the body suffers disharmony and becomes diseased. Un-
controlled emotions are enemies of health as well as peace.

According to ancient Hindu psychology there is a desire-
body called the *kamarupa*, which is enmeshed with the physical
body. The Creator gave us this to serve us during our lives on
earth. It was meant to be a servant, but with most human beings, it has become the master. Bringing us excitements, and all
the lusty pleasures of sensual enjoyment, the kamarupa enslaves
our minds and bodies. It lives our lives for us.

When we have remembered our Spiritual Home and, like
the Prodigal Son, set our feet on the Path toward it, we must

come to terms with the kamarupa. We will still, of course, have certain necessary instinctive desires and needs, such as the desire for food, shelter, and good health, but the whole bagful of superfluous, damaging desires must be exchanged for one desire. Swami likens this to changing the weight of many heavy coins for one light banknote. The one unburdensome banknote is the desire to reach the eternal Divine Shanti—the "Promised Land" of Peace. This "currency exchange" is not an immediate process. It takes place gradually by following the guidelines, or lead lights, of Prema, Satya, Dharma and Shanti.

Though Shanti is a result of the other three, we can strive to gain it directly by aiming to keep an equal-mindedness in all situations, and by progressively cutting the cords that attach us to worldly things. Possessiveness, clinging attachment, is the cause of many fears, worries, jealousies, and other enemies of Peace.

We must, therefore, try to understand that in this life we own nothing. All our so-called possessions we hold in stewardship from God, and the moment will surely come when He will take them all away—either through death or by some other circumstance. We must, of course, as good stewards, take care of all that He has put in our charge, but keep always in mind that nothing of this world is really ours.

"Once you have acquired this attitude of unaffectedness and non-attachment," says Swami, "you will have unshakeable Shanti, self-control and purity of mind."

Right from the beginning, the four guidelines must be used like lighthouses. They are all constantly there, shining beacons to keep us on course. Yet there is one light that is more important than the others. It gleams the brightest of all in the dark night, to hold us safely on the Sai course. That one is Prema.

Swami says, "The fuel Prema yields the divine flame of Shanti. Prema brings about (the) unity of all mankind, and this unity, combined with spiritual knowledge, will bring about world peace."

CHAPTER EIGHT

Meditation

LIFE'S OUTER JOURNEY, guided by the Sai lamps of love, truth, duty, and peace, finds help and inspiration by regular expeditions along an inward journey, taken through prayer and meditation. Both prayer and meditation are attempts to commune directly with God, or with our higher Self, however we prefer to regard it. Prayer, being verbal, is the easier. And when sincere, it raises the consciousness above the mundane ego, and is effective. Meditation, transcending the obstacles of the mind, brings us closer to the Divine Self, transforming our character and life. Both prayer and meditation should be practiced regularly.

For meditation, Sai Baba gives general rules that anyone may follow. No one will go wrong in taking them as basic guidelines and, through experience and experiment, adapting them to his or her own needs and nature—for meditation is a highly individual art. Individuals who are near Swami, and look to him as a sadguru, will, if necessary, be given individual instruction by him. But his general rules are for the guidance and help of all. He has enunciated and explained them from time to time to different groups and crowds, and all words given below in quotation marks are Swami's words.

We cannot know God without first knowing ourselves, Swami explains. So we must dig down into the core of ourselves

in order to reach the core of God at His greatest—which is
the object of meditation. We must dig through the ego-con-
sciousness, through the muck-heap of selfish desires, through
the hurdy-gurdy of the mind. It sounds like a big operation, and indeed, it is! But not impossible, because there is a
tried and tested know-how for it. All we need is the will, the patience, and the determination to give it a fair trial for ourselves.

"Set aside a few minutes every day at first for this, and later
go on extending the time, as and when you feel the bliss you get
from it."

The posture for meditation must be comfortable, steady,
and relaxed while sitting upright, either on a mat or in a
straight-backed chair. If you stand, you will too soon grow tired;
if you lie down, you will probably fall asleep. Even so, some individuals do meditate successfully in the standing or prone posi-
tions. But neither are advised as a general rule.

After first ensuring that the body is fully relaxed in a sitting
posture, the next step is to withdraw attention from the field of
the five senses, which generally keeps the thoughts jumping
from place to place like a monkey on a tree. By closing the
eyelids lightly, you can deal with the sense of sight. But some of
the other senses are not so easy to block off. Nor is the mind's
eye, with its continual procession of images.

A good way to overcome all the distractions of the senses,
and the mind, is to recite inwardly a *mantra* (or verse) on the
glory of God. By concentrating wholly on this (and its meaning)
in the depths of the mind, you raise your consciousness to a
higher level, and the distractions of the mundane world fall away.

Instead of a mantra, a name of God can be used. This
practice is called *japam*. While repeating the Name, any name
dear to the heart, draw before the mind's eye the form which it
represents. "When your mind wanders away from the recital of
the Name, take it onto the picture of the Form. When it
wanders from the picture lead it to the Name. Let it dwell either
on that sweetness or this. Treated thus, it can be easily tamed.
The imaginary picture you have drawn will be transmuted into

the Emotional Picture dear to the heart and fixed in the memory. Gradually this will become a true vision as the Lord assumes the Form in order to fulfill your desire. This is the best kind of *dhyana* (meditation) for beginners."

Do not get discouraged, Swami adds, if you are not able to concentrate long at first. He likens the problem to learning to ride a bicycle. At first we find great difficulty in keeping our balance on the bicycle, but after practice we can negotiate it easily, even through crowded thoroughfares. So, too, practice will enable us to maintain the concentration necessary for meditation in the most difficult situations, for long periods. So the secret is to keep up regular practice.

If beginners find that meditation on the Name and Form does not suit them, there is another type that can be used. Swami calls it a "universal and effective form" of meditation.

After taking the correct posture and relaxing the body, look steadily at the flame of a lamp or candle in front of you. The flame should be quite still. Understand it to be the symbol of the Divine Light that shines with an everlasting effulgence. It is the golden glory of God that radiates through all the atoms of creation. It is, therefore, a very suitable subject for meditation. To begin with look as long as you can, or as long as you wish, at the glowing flame, concentrating on its form and deepest symbolic meaning. Then lightly close your eyes and visualize the flame inside you, between your eyebrows.

Then, "Let the Light slide down into the lotus of your heart, illuminating the path. When it enters the heart, imagine that the petals of the heart open out one by one, bathing every thought, feeling, and emotion in the Light, and so removing all darkness from them." Now picture this pure Light going into every part of your body. At first this will be simply an exercise in imagination, but in time you will see the real Light whelming every cell in your body, every corner of your mind. The Light will purify and harmonize your whole being.

But you do not keep the Light to yourself. "Let it spread from you in ever widening circles, taking in your loved ones, your kith and kin, your friends and companions, nay, your enemies and rivals, in fact all men and women wherever they are, all living beings, the entire world." You will thus become one with the Divine Light that embraces all.

Swami also teaches and recommends a meditation that is a combination of the above two; that is, you combine meditation on God-with-Form and on the Light, or God-without-Form.

"If you are adoring God in any Form, try to visualize that Form in the all-pervasive Light. For Light is God and God is Light." After concentrating for a time on the beloved form in the center of the lambent light, you may let the Form merge in the Light, while remembering that God is not confined to a form, and is really better represented by clear pure light. Though the form vanishes, the light will itself be suffused with the Divine Excellences that were felt in the Form—Love, Joy, Power, Truth and Peace. The Divine Light is not impersonal.

Whatever the type of meditation used, when it is over, do not jump up suddenly. You have been in an altered state of consciousness, and it is better that you return from it slowly, gradually, in a leisurely way. Then stretch your limbs, stand up easily, and enter upon your usual duties.

During these duties, bring back into memory from time to time the joy and new awareness you experienced through meditation. That joy and awareness should change your attitude toward everyone and every situation. "Meditation without compassion is a negation of religion. Spirituality without love is an exercise in futility. Your thoughts, words, and deeds should be inspired by pure, selfless love."

In other words, meditation is not something to be performed for half an hour, or so, and then forgotten. It is something that should impregnate your daily life, bringing a constant sense of unity, love of all life, and governing your actions accordingly. Though you cannot spend all your time on the inward journey, you should let the interior life illumine and direct the exterior life.

Swami often points out, incidentally, that the technique we call meditation is not the same as concentration. It is important to remember this whatever your chosen technique. Concentration is a preliminary exercise to meditation. But when you move into the meditation itself, you are in a state of relaxed but alert awareness. Someone aptly likened it to sitting in a silent room alone. You are not expecting anything to happen, but you are alert in case it does. If anyone enters the imaginary room it may be through any of several doors, so you do not concentrate on any entrance; you simply wait in utter quietude.

When in this quietude of mind you forget that you are meditating, then you really begin to meditate. Expecting, trying to bring about some result will frustrate the result. High, suprasensual or spiritual experiences are always something "given." We can only prepare ourselves to receive them.

With time and practice, meditation will merge into samadhi which is its culmination and goal. "Samadhi is the ocean to which all sadhana (spiritual exercise) flows. Every trace of Name and Form disappear in that ocean . . . There is the Self alone, nought else—that is samadhi. If there is aught else, it cannot be samadhi."

The whole of the searcher's life should be employed in a campaign to come closer to God. In this campaign a regular period of meditation, using the tested techniques for breaking down the barriers between ourselves and God, is a great help. Meditation sessions are not something separate, but rather they are the high points of the spiritual life.

Different religio-philosophic and spiritual groups have given different meditation techniques, and Swami, himself, has taught other methods for more advanced pupils. But they are all built on the same basic Raja Yoga principles for achieving samadhi. They all entail correct posture, control of the body, the senses, the mind, and one-pointed concentration of attention, leading on to the beyond-thought states of meditation and samadhi.

Swami's meditation method is devotional, raising the heart and consciousness through the inspiration of love. Its techniques are, therefore, very suitable for all on a *bhakti* path, and particularly for those on the Sai Path—which places bhakti, or devotion, first.

Not only are all meditation methods one in purpose and basic principles, but the same can be said of all religions. Religion, by the derivation of its name (*re*, back and *legare*, to bind), aims to bind man back to God. Whatever its outward practices, rituals, and formulated creeds, the inner purpose of every religion is, like its daughter, meditation, to bring us back to God and unite us again to the Divine Source.

Swami is constantly teaching this great inner unity of all religions. "There is only one religion," he says, "the religion of the heart – the religion of Love."

God, he says, is like the goldsmith buying religious idols and statues. Whatever the figure – Krishna, Christ, Shiva, the Buddha, or others – the goldsmith pays only for the weight of gold in each. He cares nothing for the religious figures, themselves.

In the same way, "God weighs up what is in our hearts, not whether we have followed this form or that, this teacher or that, this faith or that. It is the quality of our hearts that matters."

If Baba's "religion of the heart" lies at the base of all religions, their fundamental teachings should be the same as Swami's teachings and the same as each other. Whatever differences there are should be superficial and unimportant to the main issue. In the next few chapters, let us compare the teachings of some of the main religions with those of Sai Baba. In this way we may succeed in extracting the essence of religion, itself, and find the universal heart-religion of mankind.

CHAPTER NINE

Sai Baba and Christ

BROUGHT UP AS a Christian and always greatly interested in the New Testament, I see many fascinating parallels between Sai Baba and Christ. These lie in the whole spectrum of their lives, teachings, and work for humanity, but are particularly obvious in certain aspects of it.

Miracles

The miraculous powers of both belong to their Divine Natures. The great power of healing flows as generously from Sai Baba as it did from Christ. In neither case did it matter whether the sick person was close at hand or many miles away. If patients have the faith to receive the power, they are healed wherever they might be.

Christ used to say, "Go your way and sin no more." Baba says the same thing in different words. He points out that, to be free of disease we must cleanse our inner natures, and put right our ways of thinking.

Both the Godmen, as well as curing the "incurable," have brought people back from the "dead."

Revealing his power over the atoms and molecules, Jesus turned water to wine at a wedding feast at Cana. He seems to have done this sheerly through kindness to an embarrassed host.

As told in an earlier chapter, Baba has, on several occasions, transmuted water into petrol. He also once changed river water to fruit juice to please a busload of thirsty devotees. But the transmutations of both the Godmen have been done only in rare, specific situations. Neither has juggled with the molecules of Mother Nature enough to upset her steady economy.

Both Christ and Baba have also multiplied quantities of food when necessary, out of kindness to people. Bible students know well the stories of how Christ increased small quantities of food to feed thousands. He seems to have done this on at least two occasions. Baba has done the same thing a number of times.

Once, incidentally, his motive—like that of Jesus at Cana— seems to have been to save a hostess' painful embarrassment. He was, on this occasion, invited to a wedding feast at the home of a very poor family in Puttaparti. The bride's mother had prepared food for the few guests she could afford to have. As Baba was expected, she awaited his arrival before serving the food.

When he arrived, she was appalled to see that he was bringing about a hundred of his followers with him. She was so shocked and embarrassed that, not knowing what to do, she went and hid behind a door. Swami quickly found her and told her to start serving the food as all the guests were waiting. She explained, tearfully, that she did not have enough to go around. Swami smiled gently, and said, "Just put out the leaves and start serving what you have."

She spread the plantain leaves that serve as plates, and returned to the containers of food. Swami came and touched the food, saying *akshaya* (which means "unending").

"Now serve the food without fear," he told her.

She did so, and found to her joy that there was plenty for everyone.

One of the hundred extra guests whom Swami brought to the feast was Nagamani Purnaiya of Bangalore who later told me the story.

Love

Jesus Christ is often called the Prince of Love, and Sai Baba is known as the Embodiment of Love. In Baba's presence we feel Love emanating from him, and when we go away, that Love still surrounds and fills us. Those near to Christ in his lifetime must assuredly have felt the same aura of Love, and even now, so long afterward, the Christ Love still stirs the hearts of his sincere devotees.

Through the centuries, Christ's saintly devotees have written the hymns that express so well the way of devotion, faith, and self-surrender, which is the Christian path, and also the Sai path. The words of the Christian hymns, I feel, apply equally to Baba. Only the name has to be changed and, as Swami teaches, God has a thousand Names and responds to any and all of them.

In the spirit of the *bhakti marga* (the path of devotion), the hymns depict God as friend, parent, master, lover, shepherd, and redeemer. In whatever role our love places God, he responds accordingly. This great truth of the bhakti marga was taught by the ancient sage Narada in his *Bhakti Sutras*, and it is demonstrated by Sai Baba in his life. Different eyes see him in all the various roles mentioned by Narada and sung in the Christian hymns.

Christ taught that we must love our enemies, and he forgave even those who crucified him. Baba teaches the same and also sets the example. For instance, he forgives those who write slanderous lies about him; he forgave those who tried to poison him (on two occasions) and, early in his life, those who tried to burn down the hut in which he was living. It is understood by his true devotees that Swami loves all—those who hate him as well as those who love him.

The essence of both the Christian and the Sai teachings is love of all people and all life. Today, for this scientific age, Swami teaches the basic reason for this universal love—the Vedantic truth that we are all parts of the One Whole. It is the nature of the parts to be drawn toward the Whole and toward each other. They all belong together, and will eventually come into harmonious union again. Attraction not repulsion, and therefore love not hate, is the law of our nature.

Parables and Karma

Both of the great Teachers use the parable copiously. For the multitudes Jesus wrapped up the deepest spiritual truths in the form of parables, from which meanings could be drawn at different levels of human understanding.

Sai Baba uses the parable, or illustrative story, just as much, but in a somewhat different way. He states the deep spiritual truth directly, and uses the parable to illustrate it. Does this, perhaps, indicate that there is a higher level of spiritual understanding now than there was in the days of the ancient Roman Empire?

There is another striking, and rather unexpected, similarity in the way both teachers deal with the law of karma, or compensation—the law which states that mankind must, individually and collectively, reap the harvest of good and bad deeds done.

In general, Hinduism and Buddhism tend to teach this as an inexorable moral law from which there is no possible escape. Every wrong act or word or thought will inevitably bring its result in suffering. There is no remission, no mercy, in the law. It works as impersonally, as relentlessly, as a law of mechanics. Only by such a law, they teach, will people learn to live rightly.

While Christ also taught that we reap as we sow, and will suffer for our sins, he offered a way out. It was this: if people confess their sins, truly repent and resolve to sin no more, they will be forgiven. They will be redeemed and will not suffer the karmic consequences of their acts. All people, of course—with the possible exception of some saints—continue to sin, that is to commit errors, as long as they live. Hence the confession, the repentance, the intention to sin no more, and the prayer for forgiveness must be a continuing process. Yet, in itself, this is a process that brings one closer to God, and by His grace the awful results of one's wrong living can either be remitted or eased. We are, in this way, helped off the wheel of karma.

As Sai Baba was born a Hindu, one might expect his explanations and interpretation of karma to be, in general, the same as those of Hinduism. But, in fact, the essence of his teaching on this subject seems nearer to that of Christ. Even so, he emphasizes the operation of the karmic law more than Christ did. He teaches that we live many lives on earth, whereas Christ does not seem to have done so. Incidentally, Christ did not deny the doctrine of reincarnation whenever the concept was alluded to in his presence, but, on the other hand, the scriptures do not show him expounding it.

Baba teaches that the fruits of our actions may be gathered in this life or in later lives. The karmic law has little respect for time. This is because our deeds, thoughts, and desires create certain karmic tendencies within us. From these will sprout either the thorns of suffering, or the heavenly fruits of joy. The thorns can only be eliminated by eradicating their roots—wrong karmic tendencies.

These roots lie deep and, generally can only be removed by hard lessons learned, and suffering, on the wheel of births and deaths. Yet their removal can, Swami teaches, be wrought more quickly through sadhana (spiritual practices). Such sadhana includes facing up to our faults and striving to change ourselves for the better, prayer to God for help in this, and the surrender of our egoic will to the Divine Will. These are very like the Christian requirements for redemption. Both Baba and Christ state that, through such spiritual practices and sacrifices, the grace of God will come to the aspirant, and that this is the most important thing of all for salvation.

We can look at it another way. When an eminent Christian preacher said, "Christ is greater than karma," I feel sure he meant that when the Christ (Divine Self) is resurrected within the person after the crucifixion of the lower ego, past karma is wiped out. A new person is born, and the accumulated karma belonging to the old person no longer operates. But such redemptions are gradual, rather than sudden.

These ideas are in keeping with Swami's teachings, which are that the more we live in harmony with our own true Divine Centers, the more are our bad karmic tendencies rooted out. Any remnants of such karma are then made easier to bear through the grace and mercy of God.

The God of Love has no desire to punish. Suffering is indeed necessary so we can learn our lessons and grow toward perfection. But as progress is made, the suffering is eased. When the Light dawns fully, suffering is no more. This is the message of both Christ and Sai Baba.

The *Sadguru*

When Christ said, as stated in the Bible, "I am the door: by me if any man enter in, he shall be saved" (John 10:9) and also, "I am the way, the truth and the life; no man goes to the Father except by me," he was surely speaking as a *Sadguru* — one who takes his followers all the way to God.

Some Christians take the words to mean that no one can reach God except through Jesus, personally. But can any reasonable person accept such a narrow interpretation of a great spiritual teacher's statement? If the statement has not been twisted by scriptural writers, it must have a broader meaning, such as: no one goes to God except by the help of an Enlightened One.

There is considerable concurrence with such a statement. All Sadgurus have said or implied that it is difficult, if not impossible, to reach God except by the guidance of one who has also reached the goal and is fully aware of oneness with the Divine.

At Shirdi, speaking as a Sadguru, Sai Baba said, "I will take my flock all the way to God." Lesser teachers may take their pupils part of the way, but only the Sadguru can take them all the way. Both Christ and Sai Baba speak as shepherds who gather their flocks of believers, and take them right to the end of the journey, opening the very door to the Divine Presence. But neither of them is the only Sadguru Shepherd.

Today Satya Sai Baba says that his life is his message. Not only the words he speaks, but also, and perhaps even more, his life of Truth and Love constitutes his message, and points the way to God and life eternal. Thus he, too, could be called "The Way, the Truth and the Life."

But Swami has never said that his name and form provide the only doorway. There is but one God, he often states, and any of God's Names and Forms, sincerely worshipped, will take you to the spiritual goal.

Vedanta in Both

Swami teaches that the first step on the way to God is dualistic. In order to practice the path of devotion—the easiest approach to God—we must think of Him as a separate Being, and worship Him as such. This dualistic approach will eventually lead us to the inner Divine Self which we will know to be part and parcel of the Divine. From this position, the ultimate concept will finally be realized; we will know that there is naught but God, and each of us is He. The part has, paradoxically, become the Whole.

Such concepts, beyond the very axioms of thought, are not easy for human consciousness to grasp. So while we might concede their ultimate truth, philosophically, we pursue the spiritual goal along the dualistic, or qualified dualistic, paths in the happy fields of bhakti (devotion).

In terms of Vedanta, Christ also taught *dvaita, visishtthadvaita* and *advaita*—that is, dualism, qualified dualism, and nondualism. He prayed to God as the Father, a separate Being, and taught us to do so. Yet he also told his followers that they were sons of God. In essence, sons are one with the Father, and so this concept represents a qualified non-dualism. At times, too, Christ made statements like, "I am in the Father and the Father is in me, and you are in me, just as I am in you," and, "The Father and I are one," which is the non-dualistic understanding, where God is the One without a second.

Both Christ and Sai Baba cut the cloth of their teachings to the measure of the pupils: dualism for the majority; non-dualism for those more deeply philosophical. We must understand that no philosophy contains the whole truth; each is only a partial statement of it. So even the more advanced, who feel that non-dualism is closer to the ultimate Truth, whatever that may be, often prefer dualism in practice. Paramhansa Ramakrishna put the matter succinctly when he said that he preferred to taste the sweetness of the sugar rather than become the sugar.

Christian Symbols

Features of the Christmas celebrations at Prashanti Nilayam usually include some carol singing by Western devotees, speeches by Sai devotees of Christian background and, the highlight, a revealing discourse by Swami on some aspect of the Christian story.

Christmas at the ashram is always a simple, purely spiritual event—as it should be everywhere. I have heard Christians say that a Yuletide spent in the presence of Sai Baba was the most sacred one of their lives.

But at any time in the year Baba materializes Christian symbols, such as pendants bearing the figure of Christ, and on one occasion—for John Hislop—a crucifix made of ancient wood. Sometimes a pendant will have Christ on one side and Sai Baba on the other, thus teaching the important Sai lesson about Divine names and forms.

One Australian devotee saw a cross hanging on Swami's neck, though friends nearby in the crowd did not perceive it. This was a one-to-one manifestation—as it was also when a

Western woman saw Baba's face momentarily change to that of Jesus.

The experience of one who calls himself a confessed Christian, Lawrence Galante of New York, is interesting in connection with this comparison. Galante was at the ashram during the Christmas season of 1976 and was asked by Swami to speak to a crowd of some twenty thousand on Jesus Christ. From that day on, Galante says, his mind was filled with visions of the life of Christ. He believes that Baba brought about these visions, which went on for about a month.

Galante's talk on Jesus was followed by a discourse by Baba in which Galante quotes him as stating that "Christ was a Divine Incarnation. . . . Jesus was the messenger of God, the Son of God and one with God." I have heard Swami state these same concepts at other Christmas festivals.

The effect of his visit to Prashanti Nilayam was to make Lawrence Galante a better Christian. He says, "I received confirmation from Sai Baba that Jesus truly was my God, and that Sai Baba was my Divine Teacher who would take me to Him." Galante returned to America to write his thesis on "Sai Baba: Contemporary Mystic, Master and God" for his degree at a university in New York.

Some Teaching Parallels

Rules of conduct and maxims for living the spiritual life are given daily by Sai Baba, as they were by Jesus. Though they differ in phraseology, they are the same in content. Indeed, this is not surprising as such spiritual guidance is based on the Ancient Wisdom that existed long before the time of Jesus. To suit the period in which he lived, Christ gave out part of that Wisdom in a style, with the imagery and emphasis, that would find acceptance by millions in his era. Though basically the guidance is the same now, there are bound to be some changes in emphasis and some deepening of interpretations for the era at which Sai

Baba's teaching are aimed. For, as Tennyson wrote, "Yet I doubt not thro the ages one increasing purpose runs, And the thoughts of men are widened with the progress of the suns."[1]

Swami emphasizes and re-emphasizes the truth about God's immanence in mankind, and that the inner God is, in fact, our real Self. In the Christian Gospels, as they have come down to us, we do not find Jesus stressing this great truth to people. But he does teach it. By saying "I and the Father are one" (John 11:30), and "I am in you," he is stating, by inference, "God is in you." He also puts this concept in another way when he says, "The Kingdom of God is within you" (Luke 17:21).

St. John reports Christ as saying to a group of doubting, hostile Jews in Solomon's porch of the temple, "Is it not written in your law! I said, Ye are gods?" (John 11:34). In Psalm 82, we read, "Ye are gods; and all of you are children of the Most High."

In the ancient papyrii discovered in Egypt at the turn of this century, known as the Oxyrhynchus Sayings of Jesus, this teaching is put more strongly: "Whosoever knoweth himself shall find it (the Kingdom of God within). And having found it, ye shall know, yourselves, that ye are in God and God in you." The papyrii were written in the third century A.D. – as early as the writing of some of the other Gospel stories.

St. Paul, the apostle of Christ, stated the same eternal truth in these words, ". . . ye are the temple of God, and that the spirit of God dwelleth in you" (I Corinthians 3:16). To the Christian mystics this was a revealed truth, of which they wrote in different ways.

But the Church leaders lost the doctrine, or dropped it – as, perhaps, being unsuitable for the common person. Moreover, history shows that the Church establishment severely punished those who taught this most important revelation about the nature of human beings.

Finally, here are some of the parallel teachings on the theme of spiritual ethics, expressed in very similar ways.

---

[1] Alfred Lord Tennyson, "Locksley Hall," stanza 69.

Sai Baba: Whatever you feel should not be done to you by others, avoid doing such to them.

Christ: Whatever you would that man should do to you do you even so to them.

Sai Baba: Instead of searching for others' faults, search for your own faults; uproot them, throw them off. Whatever people say about any faults that you know are not in you, do not feel for it. As for the faults that are in you, try to correct them yourself, even before others mention them. Do not harbor anger or vengeance against persons who point out your faults; do not react by pointing out their faults, but show your gratitude to them. It is good to know your faults.

Christ: Why beholdest thou the mote that is in thy brother's eye, but considerest not the beam that is in thine own eye?

Or how wilt thou say to thy brother, Let me pull out the mote out of thine eye; and, behold, a beam is in thine own eye. Judge not that ye be not judged.

Sai Baba: Develop *satya* and *prema* (truth and love) and then everything will be added unto you, unasked.

Christ: Seek ye first the Kingdom of God, and his righteousness, and all these things shall be added unto you (Matt. 6:33).

Sai Baba: All are your fellow travelers, not only brother man, but brother brute and brother plant; not only brother the good, but brother the evil; not only brother the spiritual but brother the wicked. All are in the same stream, hurrying toward Infinite Freedom. Spread brotherliness through compassion and deepen compassion through knowledge.

Christ: Love your enemies, bless them that curse you, do good to them that hate you. . . . That ye may be the children of your Father which is in Heaven; for he maketh his sun to rise on the evil and on the good,

	and sendeth rain on the just and on the unjust (Matt. 5:44, 45).

Sai Baba: Man is not born to go in quest of material prosperity. He is born to go in quest of the Divine. You must live in this world but do not let the world live in you. Life is granted to us by God to enable us to see and attain God.

Christ: For what is a man advantaged if he gain the whole world, but lose himself, or be cast away (Luke 9:25)? Lay not up for yourselves treasures upon earth, where moth and rust doth corrupt, and where thieves break through and steal. But lay up for yourselves treasures in heaven where neither moth nor rust doth corrupt (Matt. 6:19, 20).

Sai Baba: If you approach one step nearer to me, I shall advance three steps toward you. I am happiest when a person carrying a heavy load of misery comes to me, for he is most in need of what I have.

Christ: Come unto me all ye that labour and are heavy laden, and I will give you rest (Matt. 11:28).

CHAPTER TEN

Sai Baba and Islam

HISTORICALLY, TWO GREAT religions have lived side by side for centuries with mutual distrust, hostility, and spasmodic outbreaks of violence. The two are Hinduism and Islam. Very few people have made any attempt to bring them together on a footing of mutual tolerance and understanding. Among those few the names that come to mind are Kabir, Mahatma Gandhi and Sai Baba.

Basically both religions teach the same truth: there is only one God – the One beyond all forms, beyond all names, images, and attributes that the mind can ascribe to Him. The main difference between the two religions is this: Hinduism holds that God can manifest Himself in any form, and that we may rightly worship Him in any chosen form. Islam, on the contrary, maintains that we should not use a form or image in our worship of the formless God.

Doubtless the Islamic idea in this is that, by seeing God in a form, many will tend to restrict the omnipresent Deity to their own particular chosen form, and reject other God-forms worshipped by mankind. Hence conflict will ensue. This is, of course, an ever-present danger and has, in fact, happened many times in the sad, bloody history of the world's organized religions.

Yet the mind that probes to the heart of things will see many points at which the two religions can be brought together in mutual respect for the other's point of view. One who worked strenuously to do so was the poet-saint of the 15th century, Kabir. Although himself a Hindu, Kabir gained many Moslem followers. Indeed, he became the chief of the gurus of the Sufis, a mystic Moslem sect with a deep understanding of Islam. The Sufis placed Kabir's poems in the forefront of their sadhana for spiritual progress. His poems breathe Divine Love, which is the essence of Sufism, as it is of the bhakti path in Hinduism.

During his life at Shirdi, Sai Baba often referred to Kabir, sang Kabir's songs, and, indeed, stated that he was, himself, an incarnation of the divine poet. Born of Hindu parents, Shirdi Sai Baba had two spiritual preceptors in his youth. One was a Moslem fakir, the other a devout Hindu. When he went to the village of Shirdi to live, he took up residence in an old, disused Moslem mosque, yet his first devotee was a Hindu priest named Mahalsapathy.

The Hindus who came to Baba had to accept a degree of Islamic flavoring. For instance, Baba wore Moslem dress, spoke in a Moslem language (Urdu), and often referred to God as Allah or the Great Fakir.

One of the Moslems who came to Shirdi was a man named Abdul, who attached himself to Baba for nearly thirty years, arriving in 1890 and remaining until Baba passed away in 1918. Abdul's chief job was to fuel the five perpetually burning lamps and keep them alight.

Sitting in the mosque, Baba occasionally opened the Koran and made Abdul read passages from the place at which it was opened. Sometimes Baba would quote passages from the Koran, and Abdul wrote down Baba's utterances in a notebook. Everything that fell from Baba's lips was regarded as sacred, and Abdul enshrined it all in the book. The notebook became Abdul's Koran, which he regarded as a sufficient guide for himself and everyone else.

For many years after Baba's *mahasamadhi*, Abdul remained at Shirdi, decorating the tomb, arranging flowers on it, and receiving the first *prasad* for his sustenance. When anyone wanted help in some predicament, and asked Abdul, he would open his book of Baba's utterances, and the answer came out of the page at which it was opened. This proved effective. For instance, a well was dug at the Sai Mandir, but the water was brackish. Abdul consulted his book and the reply was: "If deeper the well is dug, the water will become sweeter." Accordingly, the well was dug two feet deeper, and the water was no longer brackish.

On the other hand, for their part, the Moslem devotees had to stomach a number of unpalatable practices, such as Baba being worshipped with Hindu ritual, and treated as an Avatar of God—a concept which the Moslems do not accept.

Such was the magnitude of the power, love, wisdom and understanding of Sai Baba that, during his years at Shirdi, a large number of Moslems—as well as Hindus and people of other faiths—became Sai devotees. Thus, throughout his life, Baba carried on Kabir's work of building a bridge between the two apparently antagonistic religions.

During his present life as Satya Sai Baba, he continues with this difficult task. In the family of religion, the grandfather (Hinduism) and the grandson (Islam) must come to a better understanding, he says. They must dig deeper into the well of truth to reach the sweeter waters of harmony and brotherhood.

Harmony and concord, he always teaches, must begin right where we find ourselves—in the home, the village, the local community. Accordingly, his work with the Moslems began in his own village of Puttaparti. During their holy month of Ramzan, the village Moslems are always invited by Swami to come to the Prashanti Nilayam ashram every day before dawn to sing hymns in praise of Allah.

In recent years Baba had a mosque built for the poor Moslem villagers of Puttaparti. Previously they had been forced to walk three or four miles to another village for their group prayers. The new mosque was completed during the month of Ramzan in 1978. Baba, himself, attended the opening ceremony, and gave a discourse to the assembled Moslems, mainly farmers, artisans and small tradesmen.

In the discourse Swami said that the Koran, which was revealed to the Prophet Mohammed during the month of Ramzan, was a Divine Communication. It reached the Prophet through waves of Divine Vibrations in the same way that the truths of the Vedas, the Bible, the Zend Avestha, and other great scriptures had been revealed to mankind. He explained that the greatness of the Koran, contained in the five principles of mercy, truth, sacrifice, forgiveness and tolerance, is also found in all the sacred religious texts of humanity.

Going as always to the inner meaning of religious practices, Swami said that the fasting prescribed in Islam at Ramzan entailed more than abstaining from food and drink from dawn to sunset. It also involved restraint from violence, falsehood, anger, envy and the maligning of other people. "Do not merely observe ritual prayers and fasts, but practice gentleness and upright conduct to create happiness in society." In fact, the abstention from food and drink should be an outward sign of the more important inward fast—that is, the sense control, and the cleansing of the spirit, that bring us nearer to God.

If the villagers assimilated the deeper truths in this precious legacy, the Koran, they would live together harmoniously with people who profess other religions. And they would set a good example to other people. After the discourse Baba materialized by his Divine Will seven silver lockets in the shape of the Arabic inscription, "Allah," and gave them to the Convenor of the Mosque Committee for distribution among the other members.

The joy that all felt in Baba's gesture of goodwill, symbolized by the establishment of the village mosque, was shown in the way the villagers—Moslems and Sai devotees of other faiths—thronged the route to the new mosque on opening day. With hymns in Urdu and Telegu, specially composed for the occasion, they gave welcome and praise to Baba.

Moslems are drawn to Swami, not only from all parts of India, but also from such distant places as Lebanon, Iraq, Iran, and Libya. They see him as a great prophet, a Divine Mystic, or they feel, as one expressed it, "that the Light that shone through all religious founders of the past is present in the person of Satya Sai Baba today."

Two of our good friends, who are devout Moslems and devotees of Sai Baba, are Professor S. Bashiruddin and his wife, Zeba. The Professor is head of the Department of Communications and Journalism at the Osmania University in Hyderabad, India, and expresses himself fluently in English on the relationship between Sai Baba and Islam. He kindly sent me the manuscript of an article he had written, titled, "Satya Sai Baba: The Divine Mystic," with permission to write of his ideas and quote his words as I desired.

In one place he writes: "I hear in Baba the meaning of the Koranic verses, and see him as the most merciful, most forgiving divine force, giving concrete meaning and experience to Allah's benevolent spirit. . . ."

And, "In the Koran it is pointed out that 'God does not distinguish between the original teachings of one religion and the other' (11:136), but merely confirms the purity of the earlier scriptures. Also, that the essence of the original teachings of all religions is the same subject, with only adaptation to local culture, geography and other environmental factors. Sri Sai Baba emphasizes that the Vedas and Puranas do not belong to India or to any other country, or even to any one religion. They are for all mankind as the voice of God (Truth). . . ."

The Islamic idea of God, as beginningless, endless, and beyond all human understanding is just what Swami teaches about the highest divinity. Furthermore, Swami says that God is present in everyone as the *Atman*; while in the Koran, God states, "I am in your own soul. Why see ye not?" And this immanent God, Swami teaches, and demonstrates, knows all your most secret thoughts and feelings. In the Koran this same amazing truth is taught: "God knows the innermost whispers of the human mind."

Professor and Mrs. Bashiruddin, like thousands of other people, have experienced this Divine Omniscience, through Sai Baba, on a number of occasions. Here is one he relates in which, he says, they "learned the hard way."

"When we met Swami together for the first time, we had to wait for five days before he called us for an interview, as we reached Puttaparti with a certain amount of resentment in our hearts for each other—probably both of us had strong egos. When it struck me that this may be the reason for Swami not calling us for an interview, we made prayerful amends on the evening of the fifth day, forgiving each other, and dissolving the traces of past grudges. The very next day Swami gave us the boon of an interview. His first remark, with a beaming smile was: 'How is your quarrel?' Realizing shamefacedly that Swami was aware of what had gone on secretly between them, they hastened to reply that the quarrel was no more."

The Professor had heard that Swami sometimes gave mantras to certain of his devotees, and felt a strong desire for a mantra of his own. It was at an interview during the Dassera Festival of 1977 that Bashiruddin requested a mantra for his personal use.

"What mantra?" said Swami, raising his hand, and, from under the Professor's shirt collar, pulling out a silver locket bearing the Arabic inscription 'Allah.' Baba had materialized this locket during an earlier interview at Dharmakshetra in Bombay. Without another word Swami pushed the locket back in place. "This convinced me," writes the Professor, "that the mantra relevant to me was already around my neck."

This Moslem devotee of Baba says that it was a crisis related to his work—and involving a loss of confidence—that led him first to Sai Baba. And although that problem is now solved and in the past, he finds that the continued grace of Baba is like an anchor in whatever hour of need may come, or for just facing the day-to-day problems that arise. His faith in the ever-present help of Baba has been intensified and enhanced by many personal and family miracles—both tangible and intangible.

The scholarly Zeba Bashiruddin is one of two Moslem ladies who write inspired poetry to Baba. The other is the distinguished Persian poetess, Begum Tahira Bano Sayeed, who feels the Prophet's spirit in Sai Baba. She has been a Sai devotee for over a decade now.

Professor Bashiruddin told me that his wife, Zeba, when she came to Swami, was a very orthodox Moslem. I know that she is a highly educated woman, cultured, sensitive, yet ever ready to perform menial tasks in the service of the Lord.

Zeba has published a slim volume of devotional poems to Swami. They are written in Urdu, with an English translation, and have a strong Sufi flavor in which God is seen as the Beloved of the human heart. She graciously presented a copy of the book to my wife. The theme of her Preface to this little volume of poetry is a Sufi approach and understanding of Sai Baba. Sufism, being the deep, true heart of Islam, is certainly the best antidote and corrective for the religious fanaticism found amongst the Moslem people in a number of countries today.

Zeba writes in the Preface: "When I first saw Baba, I was a traditionally brought up Moslem. My parents, pious and scholarly, are steeped in Islamic mysticism. My background of mysticism made me half believe in Baba's divinity. The first interview, which seemed so pleasant, also unleashed secret forces. A deep-rooted conflict began to embroil between traditional belief and the magnetic pull of love. There followed a period of inexplicable agony, until one night Baba's voice pierced my half-dreamy senses: 'You don't even know your own religion. How can you know me?' In the morning, like a schoolgirl, I turned to the study of Islamic mysticism, and when the doors of Sufism were finally pushed open, I found myself at the feet of Sai Baba."

Zeba became aware of many similarities between the Koran and the Vedas, which are the basis of the Sai teachings. She found, for instance, that two significant ideas in Baba's message are love of God and love of mankind expressed in service. "Service to mankind is service to God," Swami constantly reminds us. Zeba, pointing to the parallel, writes: "The Prophet of Islam often observed that, 'All mankind is the family of God, and he is the most loved of God who does the greatest good to his family.' "

Sufism postulates that whatever truly exists in the universe is God, and the external forms that constantly change are unreal or illusory. Baba often emphasizes this difference between the real and the unreal, and says: *"Paramatma* alone is real. *Paramatma* is Truth. *Paramatma* is Love."

Baba also teaches, as we saw, that the whole purpose of human existence is to know God and merge in His glory. For the Moslem Sufis, union with the Beloved is the final consummation. Mansur Ibn Hallaj wrote: "I saw my Lord with the eye of my heart. I said, 'Who art thou?' He answered, 'Thou.' "

Zeba found many other close similarities between Sai Baba and Sufism. All of them highlight, she says, the unity of the two, so widely apart in time and place and yet basically so inseparable. She sees also many remarkable parallels between the miracles of Sai Baba and those of the great Moslem saints.

Mohammed once commented that every saint and messenger of truth has special gifts. Through observing these gifts people are brought to believe in the validity of the mission. And so the basic aim of the divine miracle is to strengthen faith and promote truth among mankind. In pursuit of these objects Moslem saints have, Zeba says, "cured incurable diseases, mysteriously helped their devotees in distress, enriched the poor with sudden wealth, fulfilled numerous impossible desires, created objects from nowhere, and brought back to life men pronounced as dead. To me, as a Moslem, Baba's miracles exhibit the same divinity that has been manifested by the Prophet Mohammed, and later Moslem mystics."

She draws parallels between some specific recorded miracles performed by Moslem saints of the past and those being witnessed around Sai Baba today. These demonstrations of divine power, in whatever age they are performed, she states, change the attitude and lives of many people, bringing them closer to God.

Always and everywhere the powerful force behind the great diversity of divine miracles, she maintains, is Love. Yet, "The limited human mind can neither comprehend this Love, nor enlist all miracles. At best it can accept the mystic truth that Baba is the Lover, the Love and the Beloved."

Let me conclude this chapter with some lines from Zeba Bashiruddin's poetry of Love for Lord Sai.

> Quietly, without my knowing, O Lord,
> You've changed my world with a glance,
> Touching its shadowy silences
> With a gentle glow.
> The dawn now rustles down the corridors of night
> Softly, serene, unheard—
> Like the passing steps of Your Lotus Feet.
> The twi-lit heaven forever recalls
> The graceful sweep of Your ochre robe.
> And the empty moments of my crowded life
> YEARN—
> For the riches of Your over-flowing Love.

CHAPTER ELEVEN

Baba and Buddhism

AMONG THE PEOPLE of various religious backgrounds who flock to Sai Baba are to be found Buddhist priests from many countries. What seek they here, these men of the ochre robe, dedicated to the spiritual path marked out long ago by the great sage Sakya Muni?

It should be interesting to compare Sai teachings with those given in northern India two-and-a-half thousand years ago by the warrior prince, Gautama, who found enlightenment during long meditation under the Bodhi Tree. After that, the prince was known as the Buddha, meaning the Enlightened One (from the Sanskrit verb root *budh*, to enlighten, to know).

The Buddha's mission came at a time of great philosophical ferment and confusion in India. His teaching, by contrast, was empirical and practical. In fact, he avoided all metaphysical speculation.

As the Enlightened One walked through the countryside of that long ago world, observing the human condition, he saw — as he would see today — human beings forever seeking happiness, yet remaining, for most of the time, in a state of discontent, distress, or suffering of some kind. Sai Baba, seeing the same situation, says, "Pleasure is just an interval between two pains."

The Buddha knew, as all Enlightened Ones know, that, in truth, happiness and joy are the normal state according to our true nature. That being so, what is the cause of the abnormal state we find? We think that the causes of our unhappiness, frustration and suffering lie in the things around us – such things as blows of fate, bad conditions, the hostility of other people, acts of God, and so on. But the Buddha saw, as Baba sees, that the cause of the disease lies within the patient. It is rooted in desires, leading to craving for – and clinging to – the transient things of the world. Selfish desire is tied closely to delusion or ignorance of things as they really are. So a true and graphic picture of the human predicament would show us riding in a vehicle called Delusion driven by a mad driver named Desire.

Regarding this age-old human disease, Swami has said: "Divest yourselves of such things as delusion, illusion, feelings of 'I' and 'mine', and then you can be at peace." And also: "Cast away the vice of egoism, the evil of greed, and the poison of envy. When you look for joy in something outside you, remember that far greater joy lies in wait in your own inner consciousness." In many different ways Baba has stated that ignorance of the Truth is the cause of mistakes and constant self-martyrdom. If we look at the situation objectively and analytically, we must surely see this fact for ourselves.

Is there a cure for the disease? The whole purpose of the evolution of consciousness is to bring about – gradually and painfully – our elevation from the animal-human to the divine-human. When this is achieved, the delusion-born human disease will vanish like the morning mist. But is there a method of treatment, a prescription to help the sufferers?

The compassionate spiritual doctor, called the Buddha, wrote a prescription. Or, rather, he voiced the prescription to his followers, for in those days there was little writing. His followers repeated it to their followers, and so on down the generations for about three centuries. Then at last the great prescription was written down.

Would it have suffered some changes through verbal transmission over such a long period? Most likely. But at least we can check the essence of the Buddha's "cure" against those prescribed by other enlightened spiritual doctors of humanity.

The Buddha's prescription is known as the Noble Eightfold Path. It is also called the Middle Way because it steers a path between the two extremes of sensual indulgence, on the one hand, and very harsh austerities on the other. The ingredients of the prescription are named somewhat differently by different writers on Buddhism. So we must strive to see the Buddha's meaning behind the various terms used today. Here are the terms used by one writer, translating directly from the Pali words in which the Noble Eightfold Path was first set down. The first two are concerned with putting us right in our outlook and intentions.

1. *Sammadithi*, or Right View. Patients have first to get the right view of things. They have to pierce through the veil of delusion and see the human situation as it really is. They must see that all phenomenal things are transitory, that, every beginning must inevitably have an end. They must perceive, at least to some degree, that the only constant thing in this world is continual change. This right vision and understanding will help to carry out the other requirements of the treatment.

It is a view of the universe taught emphatically by Sai Baba, and it has the support of modern physics. Nuclear (or high-energy) physics has demonstrated that, behind the solid world of forms that our minds and senses construct, there is nought but a constantly changing pattern of energy. Nothing exists but the dynamic bundles of energy. The rest is an illusion created by the human mind. Even with this scientific support, it is difficult for people to pierce through the hypnotic vision of the world of the senses. So this first step toward wisdom is not an easy one.

2. *Samasankappa*, or Right Resolve. Patients, seeing correctly the nature of things, and knowing that the entanglement in the

transitory, insubstantial world is the cause of disharmony and unhappiness, must resolve firmly to control desires and cut the knot of attachments to false things. Without this firm mental resolution, and the use of strong will power in carrying it out, nothing will be achieved.

The next three requirements are concerned with patients' relationships to other people, and their attitude toward action in this world.

3. *Sammavacha*, or Right Speech. In the Buddha's time, speech was virtually the only means of communication between people. But today the requirement of right speech covers all written and visual—as well as oral—communication. We must at all times watch our words, as Baba says. Words can be poison arrows, or—more truly—poison boomerangs.

Likewise words can be powerful agents of deception, and are often so used intentionally in commerce and politics today.

Instead they should be winged messengers of Truth and Love, bringing uplifting joy and peace. At their best, written words can be immortal messengers, traveling down the corridors of time to the hearts of those yet unborn, as the words of all the great Enlightened Teachers have been.

At least patients who would be cured of their malaise must speak truly, aiming to help but never to hurt their brothers.

4. *Sammakammanta*, or Right Conduct.

5. *Sammajiva*, or Right Livelihood. These two are closely related. The first means that actions must be correct according to a high moral and ethical code. They must cause no harm to others, and, as far as possible, avoid injury to any kind of life. Ideally, all actions should be motivated by love, benevolence, and goodwill. This will be helped by eliminating from the mind all negative motivation—such things as hate, envy, greed, lust, anger, and so on.

Aspirants will be helped in achieving this ideal by heeding requirement No. 5, and choosing a suitable means of making their living. "Right livelihood" on the spiritual path means that daily work should bring some good to mankind. At the very least it should not bring direct harm to others.

Aspirants for wholeness should, therefore, examine the vocation closely to determine if it brings any harm to humanity, directly or indirectly. If it does, they should change to some other means of livelihood; otherwise the karmic effects of the work will hold back progress. Even when the nature of the livelihood is right, they should dedicate all work to the Highest, as a sacrament; then it becomes a yoga to help on the upward climb. Baba sums it up in the phrase, "Work is worship."

The last three features of the Eightfold Path are concerned with inner mental disciplines. They relate to the Raja Yoga school of the Hindu *rishis*.

6. *Sammavayama*, or Right Effort and Striving. Half-hearted, diffused effort will never achieve the high goal. Striving must be constant, unrelenting, one-pointed for this tremendous shift in our center of gravity.

Through understanding and concentration on the goal we reduce our inner conflicts; we will release greater energy and be able to put forth renewed efforts to keep our feet on the Middle Way. Sai Baba is a living example of what all might achieve through reaching perfect inner harmony. His energy seems to us to have no bounds—and perhaps it hasn't. Are there any limits when the very source of energy itself is tapped?

7. *Sammasati*, or Right Awareness, Attentiveness, or Mindfulness. The aim in this is to be fully aware all the time of what we are doing, thinking, saying. In this way, we cease to be as we normally are—automatic machines reacting instinctively and impulsively. Gurdjieff called this special awareness "Self-remem-

bering." That is, you remember yourself, and watch yourself, in every situation — as if you are a witness, objectively viewing yourself in action.

Sai Baba employs the letters of the word WATCH to help us to watch ourselves. He says, "Watch your Words, watch your Actions, watch your Thoughts, watch your Character, watch your Heart (emotions) — WATCH!"

8. *Sammasamadhi*, or Right Contemplation. This gives the direct mystical experience of Reality which is the goal of all the endeavors. But, as Baba likewise teaches, in order to reach this direct knowledge, as well as practicing concentration, contemplation, and meditation, we must live the yogic life. Every day and all day we must strive to discriminate the Truth of Being from the falsehood of appearances; we must live the life that purifies us to receive the vision of Truth; and we must go inward beyond the mind to experience the Truth of our Selves.

One timeless moment of that unitive experience will show us beyond doubt who and what we are. With further endeavors on the Path, we will reach a constant state of enlightenment, revealing our true nature of Buddhahood. Then, for lack of the fuel of desire, the fires of conflict and suffering are blown out, and we are on the edge of nirvana. Hinduism calls this moksha; Christianity calls it salvation.

The eight steps of the Middle Way are not to be taken separately, one by one. Rather we should think of them as components of a healing mixture to be administered daily. Or, by another analogy, see them as eight spokes of a wheel, each being necessary for the right performance of the other seven.

The great truths enunciated in this path were taught long before the Buddha, and have been taught, in other ways and words, by enlightened teachers since his time. Baba proclaims the same message today, which is, in essence, that we must overcome our ego-centered desires and attachments, and strive — through right knowledge, right action and speech, self-inquiry and a deep inward journey – to reach the realization of our unity with That which lies beyond all things as we know them. It makes no difference whether this ultimate goal be called nirvana, dharmakaya, Brahman, or the Spiritual Absolute.

The Buddha's teachings take us to the Hall of Truth through what Aldous Huxley called the lower door. With a bare minimum of philosophical explanation, the Buddha gave the rules for living. By following these faithfully, aspirants will eventually reach deeper understanding.

If the top door leads firstly to a consideration of metaphysics and philosophy as a preliminary to action, then we can think of Baba as taking us in through the central door where thought and action meet. He gives rules and directions for living the spiritual life, as the Buddha did, but at the same time provides much more metaphysical explanation about the Truth of Being.

The Buddha gave a do-it-yourself course in Enlightenment: "Seek your own salvation," he advised. Swami, while teaching that we must certainly do a great deal for ourselves, offers also the help of the Grace of God. He knows that the vast majority of people need something to worship, so for a time dualism is necessary for them. At, or near, the end of the long journey, they will realize that the God they loved and worshipped can be identified with the Divine Spark in themselves. But, until that time is reached, they need to look up to a figure of love and wisdom and power far beyond their own self-image. So Swami adds a ninth spoke to the wheel for the arduous journey – that is, faith in God. And, for those on the Sai-bhakti Path, the hub of the wheel is Love.

Of course, it would be a long way from the truth to suggest that the Buddha's way lacked love. Was he not known, and is he still not known, as the Compassionate One? His love embraced all life. He felt compassion not only for those who suffer, but also for those who, in their ignorance and delusion, cause others to suffer.

Yet, there is no doubt that it is easier to experience the prema, the Metta of Buddhism, the Divine Love, in the actual physical presence of an Enlightened One. The love then becomes a tangible force, an alchemical power to work an inward change, an inspiration to keep the pilgrim's feet moving ever onward. But the physical Buddhic "Body of Compassion" vanished from the earth two-and-a-half thousand years ago, and some modern followers seem to have put love in a back seat. Perhaps, then, the Buddhist priests come to Baba to experience what it is like when the Embodiment of Love sits in the front seat.

There may also be other reasons why the ochre robes appear in the Sai crowds. As far as the records show, the Enlightened One was silent on the subject of God. Yet all people long for some insight into this subject, and the Mahayana Buddhists have drawn conclusions and metaphysical doctrines from the very silence of the Buddha. These doctrines are quite similar to those of Hinduism, and the teachings of Swami, on this prime subject of God transcendent and God immanent.

Baba has seldom given a talk without using the word GOD in it. Yet, if we look closely, we will discern that what he says agrees in essence with what it is presumed the Buddha implied by his pregnant silence.

The Highest Divine Principle, Brahman, is, Baba says, without attributes, and therefore beyond all human concept and definition. Doubtless by his silence the Buddha taught this same truth. The Mahayana Buddhists believe so, and call this ineffable Principle the absolute primordial *Dharmakaya*, the Primordial Buddha, or the Clear Light of the Void.

Both Buddhism and Baba teach that the formless, attributeless Divine Principle is within everything, while also transcending everything. The Buddha stated that the true nature of every human being is that of a Buddha, while Swami emphasizes that the true nature of every human being is Brahman. So any difference is one of mere semantics.

The God to whom Swami mostly refers in his talks is a manifestation of the Formless Brahman: it may be Shiva, Vishnu, Krishna, Rama, or some other Name and Form we love to worship. The Buddha apparently did not speak of any such special manifestation of the Divine Principle. Yet in the doctrines of the Mahayana Buddhists, the Buddha is regarded as a manifestation of the *Dharmakaya,* or the Primordial Buddha.

Buddhism teaches, furthermore, that there are highly evolved beings, called *Bodhisattvas,* who have vowed to help all other beings attain nirvana before entering that unmanifest, liberated state themselves. This takes the nature of inward help to subtle levels. It means, therefore, that those treading the Path are not, after all, entirely alone in their struggle. There is aid from higher levels, though Buddhists may not call it "grace."

The relative emphasis on the factors of self-help and help from higher levels of consciousness, as taught by the Buddha and Baba, may differ, but the principle is the same: constant self-effort is necessary, but compassionate aid from above is always there, too. This great truth is expressed in different ways, and perhaps accented differently, by all the great Enlightened Teachers of humanity.

But these evolutionary, epoch making Teachers come at only widely spaced intervals. With the passage of time between their appearances, the boost they gave loses its power, and their original teachings lose much of their purity and deeper meaning. Moreover, the link of love becomes lost or greatly weakened. No doubt, as well as searching for the lost link of love, some of the ochre robed visitors come to gain a renewed spiritual boost from Sai Baba's dynamic Being, and to hear again the pure perennial teachings from a Voice of Authority.

CHAPTER TWELVE

Through Other Lamps

BRIGHTLY TURBANNED SIKHS from the Punjab, inconspicuous Jains from Gujerat, pale-faced Parsis from Bombay, and Jews from all over the world are sprinkled, often liberally, through the crowd around Sai Baba. What is the Light that shines from these four religious lamps, and how does it compare with the Sai Light?

Sikhism

While three of them are very ancient lamps, the other—Sikhism—is the newest of the world's religions. The founder of Sikhism, Nanak, was born in A.D. 1469 into an India where the two leading religions—Hinduism and Islam—were in constant conflict.

It is related that, as a young man, Nanak spent time meditating and walking in the forest. During this period, the direction of his future life was determined by a divine vision, and a timely message from God. The message was that there is no Mohammedan and no Hindu; there is but one God. Nanak vowed to devote his life to the service of that One God.

From Nanak's work and teachings a new religion came into being—a religion the keynote of which is devoted discipleship. The word *sikh*, in fact, means a disciple.

Guru Nanak, as he became known, was followed in succession by nine other Sikh leaders, or gurus, the last of the line being Guru Govindsingh. The teachings, the sayings, the hymns of all the gurus are written down in the holy book of the Sikhs, called the Granth Saheb. This book is now regarded as the Guru. A copy of it is kept at the altar of every Sikh temple, and is treated with great veneration by the worshippers.

The main features of the Sikh teachings are as follows: God is a Power and Illumination permeating all things. He is referred to as *Sat Nam* (literally, the One True Name), and is otherwise kept nameless. People, say the Sikhs, should not presume to know God by name.

The world, as we see it, is an illusion. Its true nature is beyond human conception, and therefore all our knowledge of the world is partial and evanescent. The only way we can gain true knowledge is by becoming absorbed in God-consciousness. Of the practices that lead to such absorption in the Divine, an important one is meditation on the Divine Light (*jvoti*), and on the Gurus who were embodiments of that Light.

In his first vision of God, the young Nanak was told to repeat God's name frequently—presumably the words *Sat Nam*. Consequently, Sikhism attaches great importance to this practice (known as *japa*) as another key to the door of divine realization.

Because of conditions at the time of its early development, the Sikh religion has certain martial aspects, as shown in its outward trappings. Courage, discipline, and devotion to the cause are greatly extolled.

All these basic features of Sikhism are in keeping with the Sai Path. The Light that shines is the same Light. But perhaps after five centuries the Sikh lamp needs some polishing. Time dulls the glass of all religious lamps. So maybe the tall bearded ones, in their cerise and turquoise-blue turbans, find that Swami is their Divine Polisher.

Moreover, the sacred science teaches that a book, no matter how sanctified, should never be regarded as the sole spiritual teacher. Scriptural writings cannot convey the deepest truths, and should certainly never be worshipped. Perhaps it is, then, that some modern Sikh searchers find in Sai Baba what their forbears found in the ten living Gurus.

Jainism

Jainism is one of the ancient religions of the Indian sub-continent. It is said to have existed since time immemorial, but was organized into a coherent form by Jina Vardhamana Mahavira, who was born in 569 B.C., about a decade before Siddhartha Gautama, the Buddha. The word *jina* means conqueror, and it is applied to anyone who has conquered the lower self and reached perfection. *Mahavira* means great hero.

There are some interesting parallels between the two contemporaries, Vardhamana, the Great Hero, and Gautama, the Enlightened One. Both were born sons of the ruling caste. Both left home in middle life to practice austerities. Born to be leaders in the worldly sense, both became, instead, leaders in the timeless realms of spirit. Some ancient kings of India embraced Buddhism; others became Jain.

Furthermore, neither of these religious leaders postulated the existence of a God-with-form. Both of them laid great emphasis on kindness and the avoidance of injury to all forms of life. The adherents of both religions generally have, therefore, a particular quality of gentleness.

One difference is that Jainism, unlike Buddhism, teaches the existence of individual souls, which it calls *jivas*. The jiva, by its nature, says Jainism, is free from any bondage, but it becomes entangled with matter, and by its craving for material pleasures, indulges in actions that create binding karma. Thus the jiva becomes bound to earth and subject to constant rebirth.

But the jiva, or individual soul, must free itself from bondage to matter. The way to do this, as the Buddha and other spiritual leaders have taught, is through right knowledge leading to right vision, or understanding of Truth. What is this right knowledge? It is not of the type that comes through the five senses; it is of a higher type that comes directly to the mind, bypassing the senses.

The road to preparation for such direct knowledge lies through certain spiritual disciplines and ethics, as are laid down by all religions. Truthfulness, honesty, non-attachment, non-grasping, non-injury are some of the important requirements for the spiritual life, leading to liberation from bondage.

A great deal is covered by the Jain code of *ahimsa*, or non-injury; every type of injurious action or word—from simple abuse to murder—is a sin. The Jains also lay great stress on faith and work—the kind of humanitarian work that arises out of compassion for the unfortunate.

Through the self-disciplines of striving to live the pure spiritual life, the jiva becomes, through many incarnations, a *jina*, or conqueror. That is, the soul conquers the karma created by its own errors, and becomes again a free soul. There are degrees of freedom, but in the state of perfect purity, when karma is completely annihilated, the person becomes an *Arhat*—a Perfected One, a Holy Person.

The Jain saint, Vijaya Dharma Suri, who lived in modern times, asserted that it is wrong to call the Jains atheists, as some do. Jainism, he said, accepts the concept of *Paramatma*, the Supreme Self, the Divine Spirit that pervades all things. This is God-without-form. At the same time the Perfected Ones, who receive the Jain veneration, can, I think, be equated with the God-with-form of Hinduism.

The ultimate goal of life for the Jains is the blessedness called nirvana. In this state the soul does not cease to be, but continues its existence in an absolute freedom and quiescence that cannot be described.

This nirvana of the Jains is surely not dissimilar to the Hindu concept of moksha and mergence with Brahman (also a state beyond description). Nor is it different from the nirvana of the Buddhists, of which Edwin Arnold wrote:

If any teach NIRVANA is to cease,
Say unto such they lie.

If any teach NIRVANA is to live,
Say unto such they err; not knowing this,
Nor what light shines beyond their broken lamps,
Nor lifeless, timeless, bliss.[1]

It can be seen that there is really no essential difference between the Jain religious ideas and the Sai teachings. There may be differences in emphasis, but basically the two are one. Why then are the Jains drawn to the great Sai magnet?

Any I have met at the feet of Sai have told me that Swami revealed to them a spiritual quality and charisma that they had never found in their own nominal religion. Thus he brought them back to the true religion which, as Baba says, is one. Whether the Jains regard Sai Baba as a Perfected One, a great saint, or something beyond the concepts of their own religion, they have not said. Nor is it important. An Avatar by any other name is just as sweet, and as inspiring.

Parsis: The Religion of Zarathustra

Back in the mists of time a great prophet was born in ancient Persia, now called Iran. Scholarship has not dated his birth with any certitude, but evidence seems to show that it took place over six hundred years before Christ. The prophet was known to the Persians as Zarathustra and to the Greeks as Zoroaster. The religion founded on his teachings is called Zoroastrianism, but is known in India as the Parsi religion.

It is a truly ancient religion, and, in old times, had an influence on the development of the Hebrew faith and, consequently, on the latter's offspring, Christianity.

---

[1] Sir Edwin Arnold, *The Light of Asia* (London: Kegan Paul, Trench, Trubner, 1938), p. 153.

Like most founders of world religions, Zoroaster began as a reformer of the existing religious practices he found around him. These were the polytheistic worship of many separate, often competing, gods-with-form. Zoroaster, like all the other great spiritual Teachers, taught that there is but one God. Names vary but it is the same One God. The name Zoroaster used for the One was *Ahura Mazda*, which means "Lord of Life and Creator of Matter." This Supreme Being is without form, and cannot be perceived through the five senses; He must be experienced within one's own Self. And the path to such an inner experience of God has seven aspects.

The first aspect is the understanding that the divine spiritual spark is within. This is symbolized by the fire that is kept burning in Zoroastrian temples. It is the religion's most important symbol. Through it the Zoroastrians worship the immanent God-without-form, who is the Guru in the heart, and the Eternal Fire that burns away all the dross of error, and lightens the dark corners of ignorance in the human mind. So, just as Swami teaches, the inner God was seen by Zoroaster as the most important aspect of the spiritual path.

The second of the seven Zoroastrian aspects, or facets, is called *Asha*, which may be equated with the Sai *Satya-Dharma*, or Truth-in-understanding and Truth-in-action. *Asha* is regarded as the eternal Law of God, embracing all the virtues based on Truth.

Another aspect is named *Vohy-Mano*, the meaning of which includes the innocent, loving mind and pure love extending to all life. This is the prema of the Sai Path. The fourth aspect of the Parsi Path is called *Kshathra-Vairya*, which may be defined as service inspired by love and wisdom and supported by the strength of righteousness. It is *Dharma-Prema-Satya*: right action based on love, truth and wisdom.

The remaining three of the seven facets are really gifts of Divine Grace that come to one who treads the Path. There is *Armaiti*, a name that connotes faith, peace, and equanimity. It is near to the Hindu Shanti. Another is Haurvatat, or the sweetness of perfection, while the final, culminating aspect is *Ameretat*, the state of complete bliss, or *Ananda* (Sanskrit: joy), that comes from the soul's liberation from bondage.

The scriptures of the Zoroastrians (known as the *Zend Avestha*) teach of a future life, a last judgment, and the immortality of the soul. In the later portions of the scripture is found the concept of a divine-human savior (an avatar) who will come to destroy the power of evil and establish the Kingdom of God. This may be one of the ways in which the religion of Zoroaster influenced the Jews, who were exposed to it during their exile in Babylonia, when that country was under Medo-Persian rule.

It will be seen from this brief statement of the essence of Zoroastrianism that it is in keeping with the concepts of the *Sanathana Dharma* as expounded by Sai Baba. Anyone who would like a more detailed comparison of Swami's teachings with the Zoroastrian religion should read *The Vision of the Divine*[2] written by a Parsi who is a leading Bombay dentist and Sai devotee.

The religion of Zarathustra lasted many thousands of years in old Persia, combating the ever present tendency toward a return to popular polytheism. But it was finally pushed out by another strong monotheistic religion—Islam.

Under the pressure of persecution by fanatical, militant Moslems, many followers of Zarathustra fled to India in the 8th century A.D. They became known there as Parsis (probably a corruption of *Farsi* meaning "Persian" in Persian). Their descendants today, mainly in Bombay, make up the largest group of Zoroastrians in the world. There are, however, still some small communities, several thousand strong, in Iran. Also, a few thousand in England follow the teachings of the old Persian prophet.

There are less than a quarter of a million Zoroastrians in the world today. Any growth in numbers is held back by the fact that no one can join the religion—except by being born into a Zoroastrian family. Yet, though its numbers are now small, his-

---

[2] E. B. Fanibunda, *The Vision of the Divine* (Bombay, India: Fanibunda, 1976).

torically this is one of the great world religions—a luminous milepost on our long journey to God.

The Religion of the Jews

From the point of view of religion, the Jews of today can be divided into three groups—the orthodox, the liberal, and the non-religious Jews—the latter being a mixture of atheists, agnostics, and materialists. The Jews coming to Swami are probably either liberals or agnostics in search of spiritual truth.

The history of their religion shows that the Jews are a God-conscious people, ever in search of spiritual understanding. The scriptures, known as the Old Testament, reveal the unfolding of this search into the nature and purpose of the Deity, and our relationship to Him. The Hebrew concept of God evolved from that of a tribal deity (called Yahweh), who took special care of the Hebrew tribes, to the idea of a sole universal God who created the entire universe, and who transcends it.

While in the earlier concept, God showed such human traits as anger, jealousy, vengeance, and partisanship, in the latter He is a God of infinite holiness and majesty, the perfection of moral goodness and justice. This evolution in the understanding of divinity was brought about substantially by the great Hebrew prophets who appeared regularly through the centuries, from the distant figure of Moses onward.

The Hebrew multitudes, through the passage of time, tended to fall into the polytheism of the different peoples around them. This, indeed, seems, as we have seen, to be a common tendency among people. And it exists today. Though they may pay lip service to the One God, in practice the mass of people really worship the gods of the market places and the pleasure haunts—money, success, fame, luxury, alcohol, sport, sex and others. An honest self-inquiry would reveal to us what our gods really are.

The great Hebrew prophets regularly brought their people back sharply to the One God and the worship of Him alone. At least they strove hard to do so. Worship of Yahweh meant a life of habitually right conduct, with strict observance of the divinely appointed moral law as revealed by Moses and the later prophets.

After the passing of a great prophet (most of whom had the degree of divinity that brought them some miraculous powers) the priests would take over. They would strive to maintain the true religion through regular ritualistic worship, religious festivals, and all the outward trappings of a formal temple religion. Thus, inevitably, the worship of Yahweh would become an ethnic, folk religion, rigid in its practices, lacking in spiritual inspiration, breadth and fervor.

Then the heart of the Jewish people would long again for a prophet to voice directly the call of the One God. And a prophet would emerge. In this way the spiritual "manna from heaven" came to the Jews again and again.

But in time they began to look for One who was more than a prophet, one they called the Messiah. He would not only bring the divine wisdom, but would have the power to deliver the Jews from the persecution in which, historically, they frequently seemed to find themselves. Expectation of the Messiah became very strong at the time they were suffering tribulations under Roman occupation.

When Jesus, the Nazarene, appeared during that period, some of the Jews believed that he was the expected Messiah, but the majority did not, and still do not, accept as their Messiah the person who was crucified.

The Jews still have their folk religion, and many are still searching for the deeper spiritual meanings beyond it. At least some of the Jews I have met around Sai Baba believe that he is an Avatar—which can be equated with the concept of a Messiah.

The attitude of Jewish Sai devotees is suggested in a report given to me by Ian Abrahams, a young Jewish civil engineer living in Australia. He described some of the events that took place following Sai Baba's World Conference and Birthday Celebrations in India in 1980, and Jewish reactions to them.

On the 1st of December that year Swami called all the Jews present (over thirty of them) to a group interview at Brindavan, Whitefield. Ian Abrahams, with one or two others, made notes of the interview, and together compiled the report.

It seems that in general Swami tried to lead the group into a deeper understanding of their own religion by revealing its essence, and its essential oneness with the eternal truths at the core of all religions. Comparing the Bible, the Vedas, the Koran, and other scriptures, he said that the language may be different, the place and time of origin different, but the inner meaning is the same. Yet, because through the years people have made many changes to the original teachings, we have to penetrate deeply to find the true inner meaning.

One person asked him what he thought about the Jews being called the "chosen people" in the Bible. Swami's reply was that, since all people had been created by God, all of mankind are God's chosen people.

Another asked: "Why have the Jews always been persecuted?"

"That," replied Swami, "is the level of your consciousness. You must look from a higher level." He went on to say that we do not see a reason for everything in life, but God has a reason always, and whatever God does is for the eventual good of the people.

Swami told the group to follow their own religion, but with deeper understanding. Furthermore, while keeping to their own good traditions and code of conduct with love, they should also love other people's religious traditions. Broad-mindedness, he pointed out, is a quality of all true Sai devotees because they see the truth in all religions.

At the end of the interview the Jews asked Baba if Chanukah (the Jewish Festival of Light) could be celebrated at Brindavan, as it was due to take place in two days' time. Swami agreed and said Chanukah should be celebrated at the Sai Ram Darshan Tree so that both Jews and non-Jews could participate.

"On the eve of Chanukah," writes Ian Abrahams, "the Menorah (the nine-branch oil/candle holder) was lit by Swami Himself and the traditional Hebrew prayers were chanted in His presence.

"The ritual was simple and beautiful. There was a special quality about the darshan Swami gave to all the people present. A number of non-Jews, Westerners as well as Indians, shed tears of joy at the whole scene and ceremony."

Chanukah lasts eight days and during that time the Jewish devotees at Whitefield held meetings in the college hostel with Swami's blessings. They sang Jewish religious songs, lighted more Chanukah candles, and talked about the inner meaning of Judaism, with its relationship to Swami's teachings.

"During those few days," writes Ian, "especially during the ceremony of Chanukah with Swami, we all felt that we were practising the very essence of Judaism."

He goes on: "I have thought for some years that the current form of Judaism may not be the pure form. However, I felt that it was quite safe to follow the teachings of Swami, and strive toward perfection. Indeed, we have a great opportunity now, being able to see Swami as the living example, and to be corrected and encouraged by him, while he is still available to humanity in human form."

There are many paths leading to God. Because people are different in temperament, spiritual levels, and cultural backgrounds, the different paths, the different religions, are necessary. The practice of one form of religion by the whole of humankind is not really a workable proposition.

Yet in all the different formal religions of the world there is, Swami teaches, one basic religion. That he calls the "religion of love," or the "religion of the heart." It comes straight from the spiritual heart of the great world Teachers, on whose messages the edifices of the religions are built. Whatever variations there may have been in the style and emphasis of presenting the messages by the great spiritual Leaders, the basic truth in all is the link of love between God and humanity, and, therefore, between all people. Swami exhorts us to try, while practicing our own form of religion, to find the Link of Love that unites all. In doing that lies the hope for mankind.

But there is another hope, too. While there can be no formal world religion to suit everyone in the world, it may be possible to have one religion for those who regard themselves as world citizens. This would transcend all barriers of nationality, race, and color; it would be based on the broad concept of the "caste of humanity," as Swami calls it.

Such a religion would not do violence to rationality (as some do). But it would, of necessity, be super-rational, for the follower must face concepts that exceed the grasp of the rational mind. Basically the religion's tenets would be those of Vedanta. But Vedantic philosophy alone, rational and super-rational though it is, will not stir the heart of even the most open-minded world citizen.

The heart must be deeply touched in order to turn a philosophy into a religion. And that can only be done, on a large enough scale, by a living Embodiment of Love, by One who lives entirely for the good of mankind, and has the deep wisdom to know what that good is. Such a One is, I believe, in the world today, in the form of Satya Sai Baba.

CHAPTER THIRTEEN

Sai Baba and Theosophy

MY WIFE AND I had been members of the Theosophical Society for some years before we met Sri Satya Sai Baba. After a course of study at the Society's headquarters in 1964–65, we set off to investigate whatever spiritual teachings were still being taught in modern, independent India. We thought that such a journey was not in conflict with the purpose and spirit of the Theosophical Society.

One of the founders, Colonel H. S. Olcott, said, for instance, in his address inaugurating the Theosophical Society in 1875: "If I understand the spirit of this Society, it consecrates itself to the intrepid and conscientious study of truth. . . . We are simply investigators of earnest purpose and unbiased mind, who study all things, prove all things, and hold fast to that which is good. . . . We are students, not teachers."

However, by 1965 something seemed to have happened to that fine spirit of free investigation. Certain officials at the headquarters did not applaud our proposed spiritual expedition into the byways of sacred India. One of them even admonished us: "There is no need to look outside these headquarters; all the knowledge you can ever find is here in the books."

A strange remark, we thought, from one who should have known that important tenet of the spiritual path—that books cannot contain all knowledge and all truth.

However, undeterred by untheosophical old-fogyism, we set off on our fascinating safari. We had a long list of ashram addresses, given to us by an Indian itinerant seeker, who was a fellow student at the Theosophical course, and had, himself, visited some of the places on his list. The ashrams named were scattered over the whole of India, many in remote places. So, humping our bedrolls, we traveled by steam train, by rickety buses, and by various types of horse-drawn vehicles throughout that wondrous land of Bharat, created as much by its immemorial spiritual lore as by the forces of geography and history.

We spent time at most of the better known centers of spiritual learning, such as the Ramana Maharshi Ashram at the foot of holy Arunachala, the Sri Aurobindo Ashram at Pondicherry, Sivananda Nagar at Rishikesh on the Ganges, several Radhasoami colonies, as well as other lesser known centers. We talked to *sadhus* in the Himalayas, swamis, gurus, and leaders in spiritual movements. One or two even offered to initiate us, but though they seemed admirable men, striving to live and teach the spiritual life, we did not feel that their particular paths were right for us. None of them had the indescribable divine charisma that rings a bell deep in the heart.

When we first heard of Shirdi Sai Baba, the bell rang. Even so, when his reincarnation, Satya Sai Baba, came into our lives, we spent some time "studying all things and proving all things" in the true Theosophical tradition. Finally, by some inner process that cannot be analyzed, we found "that which is good," and have held fast to it.

We soon discovered that the Sai Path does not in any way conflict with the stated objects of the Theosophical Society, nor with the basic doctrines and principles propounded by the co-founder, Madame H. P. Blavatsky, in her *magnum opus, The Secret Doctrine,* and other works. On the contrary, Sai Baba enhances the understanding of those doctrines, demonstrates them, and makes them living realities.

There are three objects of the Theosophical Society: 1) to form a nucleus of the Universal Brotherhood of Humanity, without distinction of race, creed, sex, caste, or color; 2) to encourage the study of comparative religion, philosophy, and science; 3) to investigate unexplained laws of nature and the powers latent in humanity.

Anyone who studies Swami's discourses and life – and nobody should judge him or his teachings unless they have – will know full well that the brotherhood of mankind, without any distinctions, is one of the main principles of his teachings. Not only does he propound the deep truth of this brotherhood – as Theosophists do – but he demonstrates it in all the actions of his life.

People of many nations, creeds, castes, and colors come to him everyday – continuous streams of them. He receives them, blesses them, and enfolds them in his Divine Love, and helps them in all ways that are good and wise. Through his influence and example, the diverse mixture of races, creeds, and colors around him begin to love one another as members of one Sai family. Thus is born a nucleus of universal brotherhood, with Divine Love acting as a solvent to dissolve all differences, and an adhesive to hold the great variety of individuals together.

Baba teaches that brotherhood felt in the heart must find expression in action. He encourages and inspires the organized groups of his followers to perform regular service to their fellow people by way of welfare and social work. He instructs them to look for the areas of greatest need in their own particular communities. They may find that this lies, for instance, in hospitals, or in helping the poor in some way, or in raising the level of civic hygiene, or in some kind of special education, such as training people for useful jobs.

Whatever the need on the spot, that is the Sai work that must be done. Most importantly, it must be done with no desire for any kind of reward, and with no display of ego or ostentation. The work must be performed purely for the love of

God and humanity. This Sai welfare work has become active throughout India, and is developing in other parts of the world.

I saw this brotherhood in action when I attended the Sri Satya Sai Summer Course in Indian Culture and Spirituality during 1979. The mornings were devoted to lectures, while in the afternoons the students—a thousand young men and women—learned brotherhood in practice. They sallied forth each afternoon—hot afternoons they were, too—to do whatever social service was most needed in the district around the college at Brindavan, Whitefield.

Nothing was too lowly or demanding for their hands. They often did work that has long been considered as fit only for outcasts. India was, and still to a diminishing degree is, bound fast in a caste system. But brotherhood must transcend caste. "There is only one caste," Swami says, "the caste of humanity."

As an example of the lowly work done, groups of male university students attending the course cleaned village streets and drains of rubbish and filth that had been collecting there for goodness knows how long. This was certainly dirty work for students clad in the spotless white garments that have become the unofficial Sai uniform. In the evenings the showers in the hostels were kept busy, and the dhobies were doing brisk business. Nevertheless, the Sai students seemed to enjoy this work that brought the cleanliness that is next to godliness, and showed the villagers the meaning of communal hygiene.

When heart centers are open, brotherhood becomes spontaneous. An old Theosophist, who has also become a devotee of Sai Baba, remarked, with some surprise, "I can't help noticing how ready Sai devotees always are to help one another. It's wonderful to see this practical brotherhood."

As regards the second object of the Theosophical Society, we have discussed in earlier chapters how Swami encourages the study of comparative religion and teaches the same truth as Theosophy: that all religions are one in essence. Madame Blavatsky said of this truth in *The Secret Doctrine:* "Esoteric philosophy reconciles all religions, strips every one of its outward garments, and shows the root of each to be identical with that of every other great religion."[1]

Embedded in the great religious philosophies that lie within the foundations of world civilizations is the concept of the "One in many," and the "many emanating from the One." As Baba states it, there is only One God though He has many different Names. Madame Blavatsky, writing of the many Names and many aspects of the One, says that in India they range "from *Brahma Purusha* down through the Seven Divine *Rishis* and ten semi-divine *Prajapatis* (also *rishis*) to the divine-human *Avatars*," and "the same puzzling problem of the 'One in many,' and the multitude in One is found in other pantheons—in the Egyptian, the Greek and the Chaldeo-Judaic."[2]

The attitude to science held by Theosophy and Baba are parallel. Among Baba's followers are found leading exponents of various branches of modern science. But, he certainly laughs to scorn individual scientists who think the only key to true knowledge lies in their methodology. Science can, by its methods, play only a limited—though important—role in the acquisition of knowledge that should lead to wisdom. But scientists must be humble when facing the mighty ocean of the Unknown—as, indeed, the greatest of them are.

In the pursuit of knowledge through comparative science, seminars are held at Adyar, the headquarters of the Theosophical Society, and these are attended by some of the leading scientists who are followers of Sai Baba.

Both Theosophy and Baba teach that beyond the limits of modern scientific methodology there is a body of occult or esoteric knowledge that can be tested and proved by other valid methods.

---

[1] Madame H. P. Blavatsky, *The Secret Doctrine*, 3 volumes (London: Theosophical Publishing House, 1893), Volume 1, p. 4.

[2] Madame H. P. Blavatsky, *The Secret Doctrine*.

The third object of the Society is the study of the unexplained laws of nature and the powers latent in human beings. Some of these laws and powers are gradually coming into the framework of modern science, but the majority lie beyond, in the field of esoteric science, or meta-science. Many of them may never yield to the statistical and experimental procedures of modern science.

One road, and perhaps the only road, to the understanding of the deepest laws lies in the disciplines of yoga, in the widest sense of the term. Colonel Olcott understood this, and said at the beginning that few members of the newly formed Theosophical Society yet suspected that the obtaining of esoteric knowledge, which was then the primary object of the organization, requires any more sacrifice than the obtaining of any other branch of knowledge. Whereas, in fact, he said, "A life of the strictest purity and self-abnegation, such as that of Jesus or Apollonius, is required."

Sai Baba was born with the inexplicable powers, and the nature of purity and self-abnegation that goes with them, and sustains them. Such divine powers as his are in all people, potentially. Those who live the true yogic life will, in the course of time, raise their consciousness to the level where such powers are awakened and understood. Knowledge is the fruit not only of effort, but even more of being. Until the quality of spiritual being is developed, the truths behind the highest powers latent in humanity cannot be understood.

Before I met Sai Baba I had learned of the existence of yogic powers, in theory. But one never wholly accepts a theory until it is demonstrated in practice. Through him I saw that supernormal powers are not merely philosophical speculation, but are a reality.

An understanding of the broad Theosophical movement, which began in the last quarter of the 19th century, requires some knowledge of the hopes and aspirations surrounding its creation. By researching and writing biographies of the two founders, Madame Blavatsky and the American Civil War Colonel H. S. Olcott, I gained some interesting insights into the situation, with the personalities and the aims involved.[3]

Behind the two founders were certain Adepts of the Great White Lodge, more especially the tall, majestic Rajput prince, known as Master Morya, and the Kashmiri Master, Koot Hoomi Lal Singh, who had been educated at European universities. Both lived, at the time, in southern Tibet, but traveled a good deal, sometimes in their physical, but more often in their subtle bodies. This latter is what modern parapsychology calls conscious out-of-the-body travel.

In a letter written in 1872 to a leading Theosophist, Master Morya expresses the reason for launching the Theosophical movement. "One or two of us hoped that the world had so far advanced intellectually, if not intuitionally, that the Occult doctrine might gain an intellectual acceptance, and the impulse be given for a new cycle of occult research."[4]

The heart of what the Master calls the "occult doctrine" is basically the same as Vedanta, taught by the rishis of old through the Upanishads of the Vedas. The object of the Masters was to bring this formerly closely guarded doctrine to a wider audience in both the East and West. They selected their two "front people," Blavatsky and Olcott, and brought them together in America. In New York, during the 1870s, the pair gathered around them a group of people interested in occult research. It was a keen desire to uncover the hidden powers in humanity and in nature that triggered off the actual foundation of the Society.

However, the Masters knew, as all great Teachers know, that universal brotherhood and love of mankind should come before

---

[3] Howard Murphet, *When Daylight Comes: Biography of Helena Petrovna Blavatsky* (Wheaton, IL: Quest Books, 1975) and *Hammer on the Mountain: Life of Henry Steel Olcott, 1832–1907* (Wheaton, IL: Theosophical Publishing Co., 1972).

[4] This letter is from the "Mahatma Letters," a collection kept in the British Museum, London.

the development of occult powers; otherwise the powers will certainly be misused. So brotherhood replaced occult research as the primary object of the Society.

The basic occult doctrine is set out in certain fundamental propositions in the early pages of *The Secret Doctrine*.[5] A study of them will show that they are in essence the same as the Perennial Philosophy[6] found within the foundations of all mystical writings, and Vedanta.[7] The principles of this once secret doctrine are being taught openly by Sai Baba to the crowds that come to him.

Apart from the broad principles of occultism, no doctrine or dogma was to be accepted by Theosophists. Striving to find a name for the newly formed Society, and looking at historical parallels, Olcott reviewed the work of the Neo-Platonists, the Stoics, the Hermetists and others. But the new body was different from any. "In some respects we resemble the Hermetists of the Middle Ages," he said, "but they had dogmas, and we, under our by-laws, have not. . . . We are investigators." The Society must, he said, maintain an eclectic attitude and be always prepared to investigate all matters.

Finally, the group settled on the name "Theosophy," which from its roots means Divine Wisdom. Their purpose was a relentless search for Divine Wisdom, wherever it might be found. A true Theosophist knows that this search is a continuous one, for Truth lies at the bottom of a well. No matter how much of its refreshing waters are brought to the surface, there will always be more waiting beneath.

If certain beliefs and convictions come to Thesophist investigators, through the unending search for knowledge, they should not try to force those beliefs on other members. This freedom of thought was re-emphasized only recently in a state-

---

[5] See Appendix A in present volume.

[6] See Appendix B in present volume.

[7] See Appendix C in present volume.

ment by the General Council of the Society, part of which reads: "No teacher or writer, from H. P. Blavatsky downwards, has any authority to impose his teachings or opinions on members. Every member has an equal right to attach himself to any school of thought which he may choose, but has no right to force his choice on any other."

Furthermore, in their attempt to bring some beams of spiritual light to the windows of the world, the Adepts made it understood that the Theosophical Society was not the only center through which they would transmit the Light. On March 3rd, 1882, Master Morya wrote, in a letter to Mr. Percy Sinnett, editor of the *Pioneer* newspaper in India: "The sun of Theosophy must shine for all, not for a part. There is more of this movement than you have yet had an inkling of, and the work of the T. S. (Theosophical Society) is linked in with similar work that is secretly going on in all parts of the world."[8]

The early leaders were aware of this fact. Dr. Annie Besant, who succeeded Colonel Olcott as President in 1907, wrote, "Many Masters help various Societies, for everywhere They seek channels for the outpouring of Their Life on the world." Yet, unfortunately, today some members act as if the Theosophical Society is the only channel that the Masters use, or would use, for bringing Wisdom to the world. Such a narrow, proscriptive attitude would be more likely, however, to drive the Great Ones to more humble, simpler and purer channels.

The Path used by the Adepts for their direct pupils is based on the *guru-shishya* (master-disciple) relationship which is generally called the *Guru Marga*. The Master Morya was the guru of both H. P. Blavatsky and H. S. Olcott. They often referred to him as such and his wishes were their commands. In fact, from the day she first met him in the flesh in Hyde Park, London,

---

[8] Master Morya in *The Mahatma Letters*. To A. P. Sinnett from the Mahatmas M. K. H., transcribed and compiled, with an introduction by A. T. Barker (London: Rider & Co., 1923), p. 271.

Madame Blavatsky's guru was the main motivating force in her life.

Other outstanding Theosophists of the early days likewise followed this path of complete devotion to the guru. There was, for example, T. Subba Row, a high caste Hindu and an occultist greatly admired by the two founders. His guru, too, was Master Morya. Another Brahmin, and the first Recording Secretary of the Society, Damodar K. Mavalankar, was such an ardent devotee of the *Guru Marga* that he eventually left India to go and live at the feet of his guru, Master Koot Hoomi Lal Singh, in Tibet.

With the passing of such Theosophical pioneers, and the loss of the early physical contact with the Masters, the attitude of many members has changed. They now deny the value of the *Guru Marga*, and cast a disapproving eye on any member interested in a guru, and proclaim dogmatically that a guru is not necessary. The only guidance one needs, they say, is from the books and from within oneself.

No doubt it is true that, if you can contact, and allow yourself to be completely guided by, the inner God, you need have no other guru. But, as many of the great Teachers of humanity have stated, aspirants need to be well advanced along the spiritual road before they can make and maintain that inner contact. Until then, it is easier to be guided by a true outer guru, who will eventually lead aspirants to their inner Guru. Then it will be found that the two are in reality one, that the loving outer guide is, in some inexplicable and wonderful way, a projection of the inner Guide.

Sai Baba teaches this, and also warns that there are very few genuine gurus available today. Although you might meet teachers who will provide much worthwhile spiritual guidance (I have met a number myself), it is no easy matter to find a *Samartha Sadguru* who can lead you all the way to journey's end.

So it behoves aspirants to do for themselves, in the way of study, meditation, and striving to live the pure spiritual life. They must prepare and make themselves ready for that unexpected moment when, like the bridegroom in the Bible story, the *Sadguru* suddenly appears.

The glory and power of the true guru lies in more than meets the eye, and more than mere words can convey. Understanding this truth, Madame Blavatsky established an inner group of her early followers who were ready and anxious to try to put the spiritual science into practice. Under the guidance of her guru, she instructed her group in the way to lead the divine life.

Among other things, they must, she taught, strive always to keep open minds, pure hearts, untainted spiritual perceptions, and true brotherliness to all. While enduring any personal injustice bravely, they must go to the defense of anyone they saw unjustly attacked. The ideal to which they must constantly aim was human progression toward that perfection we call divine.

The path along which Blavatsky led her pupils was called occultism, but, she pointed out, it has little to do with the occult arts, or psychism as such. In the main, high occultism is comprised of *jnana* (yoga of knowledge) plus disciplines from Raja Yoga—such as mind control through concentration and meditation—and the living of a pure life. The pure life they were asked to live included abstention from meat, alcohol, tobacco, or other drugs, and from impure sexual relations.

This last abstention included promiscuity and, under normal circumstances, the indulgence in extra-marital sex. Inwardly the pure life required restraint from judging others, idle gossip, back-biting and all activities that pander to the lower ego.

Such is certainly a recipe for the sacred life. Its ingredients are older than the Sermon on the Mount. Yet, old as the recipe is, few people have been able to bear the heat of the kitchen long enough to bake the perfect spiritual cake. The spiritual life was never meant to be easy. But "try" was Madame Blavatsky's keynote. Keep trying and practice, practice!

How like Sai Baba all this is: he, too, teaches the laws and rules for living the spiritual life. He, too, emphasizes that practice is more important than theory.

One difference between Blavatsky and Baba is this: Blavatsky, through the conditions of her times, and the cruel criticisms that assailed her from an ignorant public, organized her inner, private group. In this way she protected, in some degree, the pearls of the occult teaching and herself from the wild dogs baying around her.

Sai Baba, like all great Avatars, spurns the wild dogs, and offers the pearls of spiritual wisdom and practice to everyone. Those who are ready will receive them. Now, as then, of course, there are the wild dogs who regard the pearls as an insult, or a threat, and are ready to "turn and rend the Teacher"—as in the past they attacked Jesus and others. Their bark still sounds to-day—but, one hopes, in a more enlightened and less fanatical world.

The study of Theosophy certainly helped my wife and me to understand Sai Baba. Conversely, seeing him as the epitome of the noble aims of the Theosophical movement, hearing him expound the teachings in a new, vital way, and witnessing his life, we have come to understand and appreciate the essence of Theosophy much more than we ever did before.

In addition to the parallels and correlations indicated here, Sai Baba adds something of inestimable value. It may be more accurate to say that he brings back something that the Theosophical movement, as a whole, has lost. And that is the dimension of devotion and love. There is no doubt that the two founders, and some of the early members, possessed this wider perspective. And the Masters tried to instill it. Writing to a member of the Society, Master K. H., for example, said that he wished to draw attention to the absolute need of the "doctrine of the heart" as opposed to that which is merely "of the eye." "The moral and spiritual sufferings of the world," he continued, "are more important and need help, and cure, more than science needs aid from us in any field of discovery."[9]

Love and devotion cannot be taught by lectures, however penetrating and profound. They have to be inspired by One who has the power to set our "barn of being ablaze," and who, by

---

[9] See *The Mahatma Letters* (London: Rider & Co., 1923).

his presence in the world, can keep the fires of Love burning in individual hearts. Lacking that, what may begin as the doctrine of the heart soon becomes the cold, dry doctrine of the head. Sai Baba adds to the high ideals and teachings of Theosophy the warmth of a divine love that defrosts the heart and illumines dark corners of the mind.

Yet, even so, the aspirant has his own active part to play. For though Love cannot be created by an act of will, it can be fostered and developed by individual intention and effort. In the words of Saint François de Sales, Bishop of Geneva, "You learn to speak by speaking, to study by studying, to run by running, to work by working; and just so you learn to love God and man by loving. . . . If you want to love God, go on loving Him more and more. Begin as a mere apprentice, and the very power of love will lead you on to become a master in the art."[10]

---

[10] Saint François de Sales as quoted in H. C. Happold's *Mysticism* (NY: Viking Penguin, 1963).

CHAPTER FOURTEEN

The Divine Mystery

MANY PEOPLE THINK that Swami first announced his advent as an Avatar at his World Conference in Bombay in 1968. That might have been the first time foreigners heard such an announcement, but Baba was making his identity known to his followers in India for many years before then. In his first public speech, published in *Sathya Sai Speaks*, Volume 1, he says, "This 'speech' today is a new experience to you; but . . . for me it is not new. I have given advice to large gatherings before, though not in this Appearance. Whenever *Nirakara* (God-without-form) becomes *Sakara* (God-with-form), It has to fulfill the Mission, and It does so in various ways. But the one purpose of the re-education of Man persists, whatever the *yuga*, or the era."[1]

He went on to repeat what he had told his followers before, that during the first thirty-two years of his life, *leelas* and *mahimas* (playful and serious miracles) would predominate in order to bring joy to this generation. "After the thirty-second year, you will see me active more and more in the task of *upadesha*, or teaching erring humanity, and directing the world along the path of *Satya*, *Dharma*, *Shanti* and *Prema*. Not that I am determined to exclude *leela* and *mahima* from my activity after that. I

---

[1] Sai Baba, *Sathya Sai Speaks*, Volume 1 (Puttaparti, India: Sai Publications, 1958).

only mean that re-establishing *Dharma*, correcting the crooked-ness of the human mind, and guiding humanity back to the *Sanathana Dharma* (Eternal Verities) will be my main task there-after."

Baba said this in 1953, when he was 27, and it has come to pass. He is now concentrating very much on the re-education of human beings. The playful miracles and the compassionate soul-moving miracles no longer predominate, but they are not ex-cluded from his activities.

On special occasions, he sometimes again emphasizes the *leelas*, and makes the hearts of those around him sing with joy as of old. In writing to me about a holiday journey on which Swami took a number of his college lecturers to Kasmir in 1980, T. Nityananda Menon (one of the lecturers) says, "During the trip it was fascinating to see Bhagavan again doing so many mir-acles—picking any fruit that we wanted from an apple tree, cre-ating a variety of objects from sand, making a rosebud flower a ring for a military officer, picking up a handful of snow to change into lockets to distribute among soldiers, etc., etc."

In his discourse during the great festival of Shiva in 1955 Baba said, "This Avatar will not select some place other than the place where the Nativity took place, for the center of Its *leelas*, *mahimas*, and *upadesha*. This tree will not be transplanted; it will grow where it first rose from the earth. . . . Another speciality is this: unlike the appearances as Rama, Krishna, etc., where the life was played out mostly among and for the family members, this Avatar is for the *bhaktas*, the aspirants, the *sadhus* (ascetics, holy men) and the *sadhakas* (spiritual searchers) only. . . . It knows no worship; It will not pray to anything, for It is the Highest. It only teaches you to worship and pray."

The center of the Avatar "tree" is still where it first rose from the earth, but its branches are spreading over the whole world, and aspirants everywhere are partaking of its fruits.

Jesus prayed to the "Father"; Sai Baba of Shirdi prayed to One he called the "Great Fakir" or "Allah." But no one, to my knowledge, has ever seen or heard Satya Sai Baba pray. In this incarnation, the Avatar has no consciousness of duality. He is completely identified with Brahman, the One without a second.

At a discourse at Prashanti Nilayam in 1960, Swami gives his listeners a clue concerning the signs of an Avatar. Seven of these signs are, he said, "Splendour, prosperity, wisdom, non-attachment, creation, preservation and destruction—these seven are the unfailing characteristics of Avatars of the *Mahashakti* (Great Power, that is, God)."[2]

Even when the Divine has modified Itself to take a body, when It assumes human Appearance, these seven characteristics persist, and will be perceived by those with "eyes to see." Wherever these seven signs are found, Swami concludes, "You can identify (the) Godhead."

Many, including myself, spending time with Baba, catch glimpses of these cosmic qualities beneath the cloak of *maya* (world illusion). We see the shining splendor of his presence and of all his actions. We see the positive, unfailing prosperity of his work and mission. After a while, if not at first, we awake to his deep, far-seeing wisdom, and discern his non-attachment to all worldly ephemeral things. In his materialization miracles we witness symbols of divine creation, and later our experiences reveal that Baba is constantly creating beneficent conditions (both spiritual and temporal) for his devotees, preserving what is good for them, and destroying evil influences, bad conditions and outmoded, retarding forms.

Some people ask the question: "If Baba has divine omnipotence, why does he not remove all suffering and poverty from humanity?" Baba answers this question, sometimes, by telling the story of how Vidura asked Lord Krishna a similar type of question.

Vidura: "Why did you take part in the killing of hundreds of thousands of soldiers in the battle of Kurukshetra? You could

---

[2] Sai Baba, *Sathya Sai Speaks,* Volume 1. See the last section in this volume.

have avoided all the terrible slaughter by simply changing the mental attitudes of the chief participants."

Krishna: "My dear man, I have given everyone a sum of qualities and powers. I have also awarded each a certain amount of freedom to utilize these powers as they see fit. It is by functioning in this manner that each one can learn better. Experience is the best, though the hardest, school. However much someone may say that fire burns, for instance, until you actually burn your fingers, you will not know what a burn is."

In its broad sense the question is this: why does not the Almighty, All-loving God, through His Avatars—Rama, Krishna, Buddha, Jesus, Sai Baba or another—remove all suffering and adverse conditions from the human scene? The answer is that God has given a degree of free will to mankind. Only by allowing people to exercise this freedom of action will they learn. By self-inflicted pain and sorrow they must learn. If by divine decree they were protected against all adversity, they would never learn the lessons necessary for their spiritual growth to the level of Godman, to the Perfection of God Himself, which is their destiny.

Another question one hears sometimes is this: "Why does not Sai Baba show himself to us in all his glory and splendor and magnificence so that there would be no mystery about his identity, so that all on earth would know him to be an Avatar?"

Sri Aurobindo gave us the answer to this when he said that the infinite presence in all its unmitigated splendor would be too overwhelming for the separate littleness of the limited individual.

Dr. V. K. Gokak, who has imbibed the cultures of both East and West, and spent a period living under the same roof with Satya Sai Baba, writes, "The form of the transcendent and universal being is a source of power and a sublimating vision to the liberated spirit, but to the normal man it is overwhelming, appalling and incommunicable." Yet, he says, "To see the human form of the Avatar as merely human is to miss the conjunction of the human and divine in the manifestation as such."

But the discerning eye can see the presence of the Avatar within the human frame. Of this Dr. Gokak writes, "One catches it in the enchanting smile and in the supernatural lustre on the countenance of the Avatar, in his miraculous doings and in his aura of Light."

Sai Baba, writing of Lord Krishna in his *Bhagavata Vahini*, says, "The smallest act of his [Krishna's] was saturated with supreme sweetness. Even the sufferings he inflicted on those he wanted to punish were sweet. So no one felt the least anger towards him. . . . The reason for this was the *Prema*, the undercurrent of love that motivated all his words and acts. . . ."

From my experience with Baba and his followers, I feel that these words apply equally to Sai Krishna, that is, to our Swami, himself. Sweetness is felt beneath any surface scowl he may wear; love is sensed behind his occasional frown of anger. We come to know that true love must have its sharp pruning knife, that painful pruning is sometimes necessary for our healthy growth.

There are Sai devotees in the West who think that the Satya Sai Avatar is the promised conqueror of Saint John's apocalyptic vision as given in the Book of Revelations in the New Testament. Like all visions lying beyond the space-time dimension, the Apocalypse is couched in symbolic language. It has, therefore, been given many different interpretations by different people. But in general its theme is the return of the Godman, the Avatar, who will come as a conqueror of evil forces and establish the Kingdom of God.

In one place Saint John writes, "And I saw heaven open, and behold a white horse; and he that sat upon him was called Faithful and True, and in righteousness he doth judge and make war" (Revelations 19:11).

In her book, *The Hidden Manna*,[3] Patrizia Norelli-Bachelet endeavors to interpret the Apocalypse according to cosmic astrology and the language of the zodiac which, she says, was understood by the initiates of old. She states that the Conqueror is, in fact, the Kalki Avatar who is pictured riding a white horse in the Hindu Puranas.

Swami has not, himself, stated that he is the Kalki Avatar, but people have experienced, in his presence, visions of that evolutionary Avatar, mounted on a white horse.[4]

The Conqueror of the Apocalypse, according to Norelli-Bachelet's interpretation, is an Incarnation of Skanda (Subramaniam), the son of Shiva. Sai Baba is regarded by some of his followers as an Avatar of Shiva Himself. But I have heard Swami say that there is really no difference between the different forms of the Divine. We divide God into many deities—Shiva, Vishnu, Brahma, Subramaniam, and so on—but these are only facets of the One Supreme.

In Hinduism this One Supreme may be called Ishwara or Mahadeva, or sometimes just Shiva. In the *Shiva Purana*, Vishnu, the Lord of the preservation aspect, says to Shiva: "Who are you? Who am I, and who is Brahma? Your own three parts—you being the supreme soul. They are only different as causing creation, sustenance and dissolution. . . . You are the sole Brahman, while we in attributive forms are your very parts."[5]

When Shiva is named as the highest God-with-form, a manifestation of the formless supreme Brahman, the dissolution aspect of the *Trimurti* (the Hindu Trinity) is usually called *Rudra*. So we have Brahma (Creation), Vishnu (Sustenance) and Rudra (Dissolution)—the three-in-one, with Shiva standing for all.

---

[3] Patrizia Norelli-Bachelet, *The Hidden Manna* (Accord, NY: Aeon Books, 1976).

[4] Howard Murphet, *Sai Baba, Avatar: A New Journey into Power and Glory* (San Diego, CA: Birth Day, 1977; London: Grafton Books, 1985).

[5] *Shiva Purana*, 2 volumes, edited by J. L. Shastri (Delhi: Motilal Banarsidass, 1969).

Skanda, son of Shiva, is just another aspect of the One. This aspect is not withdrawn in meditation—as the Shiva Form is often pictured—but is very active in the world, on the front line of the great battle against evil forces.

It is also significant in this respect that, in the *Shiva Purana*, Brahma speaking to the gods says: "For your welfare Shiva himself is standing here in the form of his son,"[6] or, to put it another way—Shiva has taken on the active, dynamic aspect usually represented by his son Skanda.

Patrizia Norelli-Bachelet believes that the Hindu Puranas are cosmic revelations, containing the cycles of time, and the manifestations of divine truth, in their structure, and that the Puranic stories corroborate the Apocalypse of Saint John.

There is no doubt, of course, that Satya Sai Baba is very active and extremely dynamic. He is not the withdrawn yogi, spending his time in meditation. He is essentially the doer, the one who joins battle with the dark forces that rise sharply against the power of Light he brings.

Baba has not denied that he is an Avatar of Shiva. So is he Shiva playing the role of Skanda, his son? Some Western students of the Sai movement think so and, therefore, equate him with the Apocalyptic Conqueror, and the Kalki Avatar. If they are right, we can, according to the Apocalypse and the Puranas, expect some violent clashes of opposing forces, some cataclysmic world struggles ahead. Avatar Rama led the armies of righteousness in a great war against the demoniac forces. Avatar Krishna was involved in the holocaust of the Mahabharata War. The prophecies foretell even more terrible wars in the time of the Kalki Avatar and Saint John's Conqueror.

Even if the ancient prophecies and saintly visions are correct, we may not be interpreting them correctly. At best we are just catching straws in the wind and guessing. The cosmic language is a barrier to easy understanding and sure calculations.

Many people feel that the times call for a great history-making Avatar. But whether the establishment of the Kingdom of

---

[6] *Shiva Purana*, 2 volumes, edited by J. L. Shastri.

God is imminent, or something for future centuries, who knows? No human being can know this for sure, nor whether Sai Baba is himself the Conqueror of Revelations, or the Kalki Avatar, or one preparing the ground for a future Divine Incarnation. Only time, that weeds out errors of judgment and misconceptions from truth, can tell this.

Many rumors fly around as to what Swami has said about frightening large scale events and conditions of the near future. But when I, and others in my presence, have asked him about these matters, he has never said that cataclysmic wars, with wholesale destruction, are imminent. But, one asks, would he say so even if he knew that such appalling events were looming in our tomorrows? Such a statement from him would have a devastating effect. And, furthermore, the expectations, the powerful thought-forms of many people may help to bring about events that are not necessarily ordained.

How can we know what is foreordained and what is not? We may believe with Shakespeare that "there is a divinity that shapes our ends, rough-hew them how we will." But in our rough-hewing we may bring about dire events that are not an essential part of God's overall plan.

The Great Dramatist, like the lesser human dramatists, knows the beginning, the ending, and perhaps the main events of His Cosmic Drama. But as part of His plan He created characters with free will. Hence He will not move them about like mindless marionettes. If He did, they would be "flat" characters of no interest and, moreover, His purpose of character development would not be achieved. Like the human dramatists who follow Him, the great Archetypal Dramatist creates in joy, but He also, I believe, creates for a purpose.

If the conclusion of the cosmic story is pre-determined (and I believe it is), there are certain guidelines that the characters must follow in order that the divine end may be shaped. But, during the action of the play, the developing characters, with their degrees of free will, may often take over—as the characters do in the stories of human creators.

Misunderstandings, problems, struggles, battles, sufferings and all the miseries that flesh is heir to are brought about by such human weapons as blind desire, selfishness, egotistic ambition, lust for excitements, fear, hatred and ignorance.

Does the great author know just what His self-willed characters will do in every situation—what fantastic tricks they will play, dressed up in their "little brief authority"? The watching angels oft-times weep at the appalling tragedies we bring upon ourselves, but does the Author know in advance all the events that will form in the steam of mankind's fevered cauldron? Perhaps. Perhaps not.

But the characters in the drama are in reality His own children, emanating from His divine substance. They will grow wiser and stronger through the struggles they create for themselves in the great life drama. God loves them all—every one, individually and collectively—as Swami demonstrates. In the end, when the final curtain falls, He will bring the whole cast back to His feet—to divine Being in full consciousness and eternal bliss.

The analogy with the human dramatist may help us to glimpse, to understand a little, for, as the occultists say, "As above, so below." The truth of it all—life, mankind, the universe, God—lies too deep for the spade of thought, too wide for the cage of words. Yet the above and the below are closely interwoven, as the poet Tennyson felt when he plucked the little flower from a crannied wall, and addressed it: ". . . if I could understand what you are, root and all, and all in all, I should know what God and man is."[7]

We don't know who we are, ourselves, as Baba points out, so how can we know the mystery of God and the Godman. "No one can understand the mystery, the best you can do is (to) get immersed in it. There is no use arguing about pros and cons;

---

[7] Alfred Lord Tennyson, from a poem titled "Flowers in a Crannied Wall," in *The Oxford Dictionary of Quotations* (London: Oxford University Press, 1955), p. 529.

dive and know the depth; eat and know the taste." It matters not that you can never describe the depth and the taste. You can experience them and the joy of them.

Then, when you have sought and found the Kingdom of God, with its Truth, Purity and Love, when you have been truly baptised in the waters of that experience, "You need not even pray to me to grant you this and that," says Swami, "everything will be added to you, unasked."

CHAPTER FIFTEEN

To Look on His Face

T HIS FINAL CHAPTER is a response to questions frequently asked by people planning their first attempt to see Sri Satya Sai Baba in the flesh. To Westerners, in particular, there seems to be a good deal of mystery and many problems surrounding the operation of visiting a great spiritual teacher in India. Do they need permission? What about travel, accommodations, food, clothing? What is the best time to go? How long to stay? Where will Swami be? Will he see them? Will they get an interview? These are the main questions, so let's take them one by one.

Do I need permission? As an Avatar, Sri Satya Sai Baba is the Teacher of the whole of humanity, and the *Sadguru* of all who are ready to receive his spiritual guidance.

He has said, however, that no one comes to him unless he calls them. That call is not something you receive by mail or messenger. It is an inner call of the spirit. If you have a strong urge to go and see Sai Baba, it is likely that you have already had that inward call. It should mean, too, that you are either ready, or on the way to becoming ready, to receive what he has to give you.

Yet it seems that sometimes the call comes, and you make the contact on the physical plane before you are consciously quite ready. Perhaps he called to you before you heard, before your sleeping soul was stirred, as a hymnist wrote of the divine call.

So it is that some people are either lukewarm or resist Sai Baba outright at the first encounter. But if they give him a fair chance, it usually won't be long before the inner door swings open and the Light and Love flood in. I speak from experience.

But on the outer plane you do not need to get written or verbal permission to visit one or the other of Baba's ashrams in India.

Where is he likely to be when I go? His main ashram is Prashanti Nilayam, right beside the village of Puttaparti. This is in the State of Andhra Pradesh, and a little over a hundred miles by road north of the city of Bangalore. He has a second residence called Brindavan, near Whitefield, where he gives *darshan*. It is near the Whitefield railway station, a few miles east of Bangalore on the main line to Madras.

Most of Baba's time is spent at one or the other of these two places. He is probably in residence at Prashanti Nilayam, his main ashram, more than at Brindavan.

Occasionally he does go on tour to other parts of India, but he has never, up to the time of this writing, spent more than two or three weeks away from one or the other of his residences. You can find out where he actually is from the Public Relations Officer, Prashanti Nilayam, Anantapur District, Andhra Pradesh, India. But you can't find out for sure where Baba will be in the near future. No one, not even his own shadow, knows that.

So there is always the possibility that you will have to wait a short time in order to see him. As Bangalore is the key to both places, you can do your waiting in that city in comfort, or in Prashanti Nilayam where, in some strange way, you will be learning while you wait.

What about travel, accommodations and food? From Bangalore you can travel to Prashanti Nilayam by car, taxi, or bus. The latter means is cheap but takes about five hours and, while an interesting experience, it is certainly not comfortable. Taxis do the trip from Bangalore in a little over three hours. The road surface is now sealed almost all the way.

Many blocks of units have been built, and are being built, at Prashanti Nilayam to accommodate visitors. There is a nominal charge for these to cover cost of electricity and cleaning.

While the units have running water, toilets, and showers, most of them have no furniture, so it is wise to take along a bed-roll, sheets and a blanket. Some people take a valise containing a small mattress, some take pneumatic air-mattreses, others canvas camp beds. In any case, there are some austerities at the ashram. No one should go there expecting Western style comforts and amenities.

If no accommodation is available in the ashram itself, visitors can usually find rooms, with primitive furnishings, at one of the little hotels in the bazaar outside the ashram walls.

The only times when there is any great difficulty in finding accommodations is during one of the great festivals. The two still being celebrated at Prashanti Nilayam are Dassera and Swami's birthday. The first takes place during October for a number of days, the date of its beginning depending on the phases of the moon.

The second usually starts a few days before Swami's actual birthday, which is on November 23rd. The celebrations mostly incorporate a conference, either India-wide or world-wide, and are carried on for a number of days following the birthday. Experience has shown that during any great festival at Prashanti Nilayam, available rooms soon fill to overflowing, and thousands sleep in the open on the ground.

Indian style, low cost, vegetarian meals can be taken at the ashram canteen. Some people prefer to buy vegetables in the bazaar and cook their own meals on a kerosene stove, or some other type of portable cooker, brought for the purpose. On the other hand, some visitors choose to take meals at one of the small restaurants in the bazaar. One or two of these are beginning to slant their catering toward the Western palate.

When Sai Baba is in residence at Brindavan, Whitefield, the majority of visitors stay in a hotel in Bangalore, and travel out to see him each day. There is a wide choice of hotels, from those of international luxury standard to more modest and economical places.

Although Brindavan is right near the Whitefield railway station, few trains from Bangalore stop there. Buses passing the ashram, though frequent, are over-crowded. So many visitors do the journey by taxi from Bangalore. A prevalent custom is for a party of visitors to share a taxi, arranging for it to wait for them at Brindavan until after Swami's darshan, and then to take them back to Bangalore. The cost of this, shared by a number of passengers, is not too high.

However, visitors who do not want the expense of hotels and daily taxi rides, seem to find accommodations, usually simple and primitive, in the nearby village of Kadugodi, or in houses just outside the walls of Brindavan itself. A few stay in the small town of Whitefield, but this is not within reasonable walking distance of Brindavan, buses are infrequent, and taxis not usually available.

What type of clothes should I take? Light summer clothing is required for the pilgrimage to Sai Baba. I have never, myself, known it cold enough for winter clothing at either Bangalore or Puttaparti.

Ladies going to Swami's darshan usually wear saris. But a few Westerners, who find it difficult to cope with the sari, wear long skirts, reaching to the ankles, or kaftans, which are locally available. Modesty in dress is the essential keynote when visiting the Avatar.

Men find it most comfortable to wear lightweight trousers and a shirt, made either from cotton or a mixture of cotton and synthetic fiber. Laundry facilities are adequate and relatively inexpensive, so white raiment is favored by the majority. This not only makes for coolness but seems most appropriate. Jackets are seldom worn, though it is advisable to have a cardigan or pullover for evening wear in the cooler months.

How long is it advisable to stay? When making the long trip from overseas, or from distant parts of India, visitors should, if possible, plan to stay at least a few weeks. Dashing in to see Swami for just a day or two is not giving yourself the chance to gain the divine experience, the inner change, the upliftment of heart and mind that the Avatar can bring you. Those who go for a short visit, just out of curiosity, may come away saying that they have seen nothing but a man in a red robe, with a crown of bushy black hair. But that surely is not why you go there.

Swami may restrict your stay, letting you know when you should go, or, on the other hand, he may keep you there longer than you intended to stay. He knows best how long you need in his presence to gain what you are capable of gaining at that juncture. So, at a sign from him, be prepared to go or to stay on if personal circumstances permit — and they usually will.

Attitudes and Interviews

Go to Sai Baba full of hope, but with no definite expectations. The benefits you receive from the divine contact are nearly always quite different from those you anticipate. Especially do not go expecting to be called to an interview. The crowds that come to Swami from all parts of the world have grown to such immense proportions that the personal interview is now necessarily a rare thing.

Baba spends many hours of his long working days giving group interviews. A group may consist of a number of people who have traveled there together from a particular place. Or Baba may call individuals from the crowd and take them into his interview room together. After talking to them as a group for a time, he may, or may not, take individuals into another room for private advice and help.

Only Swami knows why he calls specific individuals for an interview. Many people have fanciful theories on the question, but only Swami knows the answer. Seeing a person's past and the problems of the present extending into the future, as he does, only Lord Sai knows when an interview is needed, and when it will be most beneficial to the person's well-being, both temporal and spiritual. Sometimes an interview may not only be unnecessary but even, perhaps, a disadvantage.

One earnest young searcher from the West sat for many months in the darshan line without ever being called to an interview. In the end he began to see this as a blessing. He said, "When Swami suddenly appears in his red-orange robe, floating towards us to give darshan, my hair stands on end. To me it is God Himself approaching. Perhaps if Swami took me in for an interview, I would see the human side of him and lose that wonderful *darshan* experience."

When a certain young woman from Australia was not called for an interview after waiting for several weeks in the crowd, people who knew her were surprised. They had thought she was so super-spiritual that Swami would call her immediately. But her own comment was: "Sai Baba is my Master. As such He will know if and when I need an interview. So I leave it entirely to Him."

This is surely the wise attitude that all should practice. Of course, it is only human and natural that people should want the more personal contact of an interview. But placing too much importance on it can lead to many unproductive, unspiritual effects. Seeping up from the lower levels of the mind may come jealousy and envy of others, a feeling of insecurity and rejection, a tendency to criticize and dislike those whom Swami calls before us.

Surely we don't go to Sai Baba in order to experience such all too familiar, harmful emotions! In fact, on the spiritual path we are striving to eradicate them. Yet they come, pouring in like water into a leaky boat.

Bob Najemy of Athens, Greece, tells how he used the trying time of waiting for a hoped-for interview to overcome such negative feelings and attitudes.[1] One of his methods was to

---

[1] See *Sanathana Sarathi*, December, 1979. This is the newsletter published at the Ashram.

deliberately cultivate the opposite positive feeling. He would, for instance, replace envy, and its cousins, with love for the people concerned, and feel happy at their good fortune.

Often it seemed that Swami helped him in his struggle by deliberately choosing people Bob had just been mentally criticizing. The shock of this would remind him of the Sai teaching that all beings are forms of God. If he felt insecurity and rejection through being ignored by the Great One, he again remembered the message that, "We are all embodiments of the Divine *Atma* and not the insecure mind." This, he said, helped him to overcome his dependence on the Form to a degree, and reaffirm his own *atmic* okayness.

Such important lessons, learned by sitting and waiting, helped Bob to do some valuable self-examination and develop patience, equanimity, and detachment. Above all, he began to realize more and more the great truth that all searchers must learn to step beyond the Form, and find the Lord within their own hearts. He concludes: "Baba will soon be so widely known as an Avatar that interviews and perhaps even *darshan* may not be possible. In light of this, each one of us would greatly benefit by concentrating more on Baba's spiritual omnipresent nature as our own inner being. Through *japa*, meditation and surrender of each act to Him, we can have a moment to moment interview throughout life."

So let us never spoil the joy of being in the vicinity of the Lord by the frustrations and inner conflicts attendant upon the "interview complex." Let us remember, in calm, meditative patience, that great—perhaps the greatest—benefits can come to us through the inexplicable inner contact of the darshan. Many have found this.

Murali Engels, of America, describing the Sai darshan and its effects on her, writes: "He ignored me completely. I should say, on the outside he ignored me, because on the inside, I was so sweetly fulfilled just to have the sight of Him so near. I was looking into the tender face of Love." And in another place: "Swami passed quietly by and went around the tree and back across the ground to His house. I closed my eyes. His face, His hair, His form still before me. Just the sight of Him was enough. I did not want to move or open my eyes for a long time. On the way home in the cab, I couldn't talk. I could only go 'in' to the sweetness He had given me.

"Upon arriving home, I climbed the stairs to my little room, grateful that I would not have to speak to anyone for another two hours. I lay on my bed, lost, again, in the love of God."[2]

Even if Swami appears to be ignoring us, he still sees us. I believe that he sees everyone who is present at the darshan. And his Love goes out to all.

The moment, the right moment, may come when he looks into your eyes, smiles, speaks perhaps. That is when many cry with happiness. No one can explain this melting surge of bliss that passes through them.

If, without expecting it, you are invited to the interview room, count that as an added bonus. It is certainly an important event, but not necessarily the most important one along the Sai spiritual path.

What we see and experience in the Presence, whether at an interview or elsewhere, will depend on ourselves and the work we have done on ourselves, for, as Jesus once said, "Blessed are the pure in heart for they shall see God."

---

[2] From an untitled book by Murali Engels in manuscript form.

Fundamentals of Theosophy

THREE FUNDAMENTAL PROPOSITIONS lie at the base of Theosophy. See *The Secret Doctrine*, proem, by H. P. Blavatsky.

1. An omnipresent, eternal, boundless and immutable Principle on which all speculation is impossible since it transcends the power of human conception, and could only be dwarfed by any human expression or similitude. It is beyond the range and reach of thought—in the words of Mandukya, "Unthinkable and unspeakable."

This infinite and eternal Cause is the rootless root of "all that was, is, or ever shall be." It is, of course, devoid of all attributes and is essentially without any relation to manifested, finite being. It is "Be-ness" rather than Being, and is beyond all thought and speculation.

2. The eternity of the universe *in toto* is a boundless plane; periodically the "playground of numberless universes incessantly manifesting and disappearing," called "the manifesting stars," and the "sparks of eternity."

The appearance and disappearance of worlds is like a regular tidal ebb of flux and reflux.

3. The fundamental identity of all souls with the Universal Oversoul—the latter being itself an aspect of the Unknown

Root – and the obligatory pilgrimage of every soul through the cycle of incarnation (of "Necessity") in accordance with Cyclic and Karmic Law during the whole term.

In other words, no divine soul can have an independent (conscious) existence before the spark which issued from the pure Essence of the Oversoul has (a) passed through every elemental form of the phenomenal world of that Manavantara, and (b) acquired individuality, first by natural impulse, and then by self-induced and self-devised efforts (checked by its karma), thus ascending through all the degrees of intelligence from the lowest to the highest *manas*, from mineral and plant up to the holiest archangel (Dhyani-Buddha).

An Outline of the Perennial Philosophy

THOUGH THE CONCEPTS and insights of the Perennial Philosophy have existed since time immemorial, the name itself originated with the philosopher Leibniz, who coined the phrase *Philosophia Perennis*. Its concepts are the highest common factor in the theologies of the higher religions, though its expression often becomes blurred and obscured with the passage of time. Rudiments of the Perennial Philosophy are found in the traditional lore of primitive peoples in all parts of the world. From time to time mystical insights and revelationary experiences bring back to mankind a full, pure statement of this timeless wisdom. The ideas and understandings basic to the Perennial Philosophy may be summarized as follows.

1. There is an eternal unchanging Reality behind this ephemeral world of appearances, this ever-changing phenomenal universe around us. The Eternal Reality has been given many different names by different Teachers through the ages. Some are: Brahman, the Godhead, God-without-form, the Divine Ground, the *Void-plenum*, the Clear Light of the Void, the Absolute, and Nirvana. But however we name it, the one and only Reality can be directly experienced and realized by human beings—under certain circumstances.

Though this infinite Reality cannot be limited in the contours of finite personality, it does have a personal aspect which is manifested, for example, in the Trinity of Holy Persons in the Christian and Hindu theologies.

We tend to think of those things we apprehend with our senses as being real, yet we know, or sense, that they are only parts of a constant flow of change. Through the long vistas of time all things have only a relative reality and this partial reality exists within and because of the Absolute Reality that enfolds them.

2. Human beings are akin to the Reality. As well as enfolding all things, It is immanent in all things, including mankind. We are, by our natures, capable of discerning this Reality. We may accept it by inference from our own and other people's inner experiences, when the edge of the great Unknown is touched, so to speak. But we can only realize and experience it fully through a spiritual faculty beyond our reasoning minds, beyond the limits of the most intense and profound abstract thought. This way of knowing, of which all people are capable, is called unitive, or intuitive knowing. It brings a direct realization of our individual unity with the Divine Ground of our Being.

3. People, in the conscious day-to-day existence, are centered at the level of the lower ego. This center is, in fact, what we refer to when we say "I," "me," and "mine." But it is only a temporal center, and not our true eternal Self, which is, in some way, part of the One Reality.

It is the chief purpose of our existence in this world to discover the true center and become consciously identified with it. But the finding of the Self is not an easy task because human beings have become deeply immersed in illusion and ignorance. It requires rigorous and constant effort, directed toward the annihilation of the self-regarding lower ego. When this false self has been completely annihilated—or changed and transmuted into the real Self—people reach a state of spiritual rebirth, a a state known as liberation, salvation, redemption, deliverance, enlightenment, mergence with God and by other names.

Names can only give a slight intimation of the nature of that state of utter blessedness at the end of the far journey to the "land that is nowhere," the true spiritual home.[1]

---

[1] For a more detailed account of the Perennial Philosophy, see chapter 7 of *Sai Baba Avatar* by Howard Murphet (San Diego, CA: Birth Day, 1977; London: Grafton Books, 1985). And for a full statement with a valuable anthology of writings on the subject, see *The Perennial Philosophy* by Aldous Huxley (San Bernadino, CA: Borgo Press, 1990).

The Essence of Vedanta

THE UPANISHADS OF the *Vedas* do not contain an orderly system of teaching. The need to systematize the teaching gave rise to the *Vedanta Sutras* (or *Brahma Sutras*). But these brief aphorisms allowed for different interpretations, and through the ages commentators have given interpretations which agree on some points and differ on others.

So there are various schools of thought based on the *Vedanta Sutras*. The three main ones are *Adwaitha, Visishta Adwaitha,* and *Dwaitha.*[1] *Adwaitha,* or monism, was expounded by Adi Shankara. *Visishta Adwaitha,* or qualified non-dualism, is contained in the commentaries of Ramanuja, and the third school, *Dwaitha,* or dualism, comes from the interpretations of Madhava.

All these schools agree that Brahman (the Spiritual Absolute) exists, and in some way is the basic cause of the universe. They also agree that knowledge of Brahman, which cannot be gained through mere reasoning, leads to individual emancipation, or liberation, which is the final goal of every being. They differ, however, to some degree on the nature of Brahman, and on the relationship between the individual soul and Brahman.

---

[1] Editor's note: Also written as *advaita, vishishttha advaita,* and *dvaita,* being more phonetically exact.

Shankara states that Brahman is without attributes, and that all Gods-with-form, including Iswara, the highest manifested form of Brahman, are the products of *maya* (illusion). The universe, he says, is also an apparent transformation, through *maya*, of the attributeless Brahman. The individual soul is, in reality, all pervading and identical with Brahman. Knowledge (*jnana*) is the means to liberation.

In Ramanuja's interpretation Brahman has a personal aspect, possessing infinite benign attributes. Individual souls are modes, or effects, of Brahman, but have existed through eternity, and will continue to so exist. By knowing Brahman, the soul goes to *Brahmaloka* (the highest plane), from where it attains Brahman and does not return to the mortal world. The world has a relative reality, and is not a result of *maya*. *Bhakti*, says Ramanuja, not *jnana*, is the chief means to liberation.

In Madhava's dualism Brahman is a personal God with divine attributes. He and the individual souls are quite independent eternal entities. Brahman is the Creator of the souls and the universe, which is real and not a *mayavic* projection. The means to individual liberation is *bhakti*. Speaking on these three schools of Vedanta, Sai Baba says:

> Monism, as expounded by Shankara on the basis of Vedic texts, was too simple a solution to satisfy the inner urges of the majority of individuals. They had in them the yearning to worship, to dedicate themselves to a higher power; they could not easily grasp the truth of their inner reality being the One and Only. Their emotions and activity had to be sublimated by discipline and devotion.
>
> Therefore Ramanuja commented on the Vedic texts and religious scriptures from a new point of view. This made *Adwaitha* take on a special outlook. So it was called *Visishta Adwaitha* (special monism). The path of devotion (*bhakti*) was laid down to take man to (the) mergence with God.

Complete surrender and (the) annihilation of individuality are also beyond most aspirants. Sugar cannot be tasted and enjoyed by sugar; you have to be an ant to revel in the sweetness of the stuff. This craving of man was sought to be satisfied by Madhava, who declared that the individual will ever remain separate from the Universal, and there can be no merging.

In *Adwaitha* a flash of intellectual illumination revealed that the *atma* (spirit) alone exists, and that all else is deluding appearance. *Visishta Adwaitha* points out that the river is an integral part of the sea. *Dwaitha* points out that the purity derived from adoration and worship is enough to draw down the fulfilling grace of God.

The doctrines drawn from the Upanishads, though they may appear contradictory, are not really so. They are attempts to express truths that lie beyond the intellectual distinctions that belong to the world of opposites. The various understandings, as expressed in the different schools of Vedanta, are relative truths that suit people at differing stages of spiritual evolution.

On this theme Swami Vireswarananda writes: "Nearly every chapter in the *Upanishads* begins with dualistic teaching . . . and ends with a grand flourish of *Adwaitha*. God is first taught as a being who is the Creator of the universe, its Preserver, and the Destruction to which everything goes at last. He is the One to be worshipped, the Ruler, and appears to be outside of nature. Next we find the same teacher teaching that God is not outside nature, but immanent in nature. And at last both ideas are discarded, and it is taught that whatever is real is He; there is no difference. . . . The Immanent One is at last declared to be the same that is in the human soul."[2]

---

[2] See *Introduction to Brahma-Sutras* by Swami Vireswarananda (Calcutta, India: Adwaitha Ashrama, 1970).

Bibliography

If you cannot find these books in your local bookstore, write to the Sathya Sai Book Center of America, 305 West 1st St., Tustin, CA 92680.

Arnold, Sir Edwin. *The Light of Asia.* London: Kegan Paul, Trench, Trubner, 1938.

Balu, Shakuntala. *Living Divinity.* London: Sawbridge, 1981.

Blavatsky, Madame H. P. *The Secret Doctrine.* (London: Theosophical Publishing House, 1893.

Devi, Indra. *Sai Baba and Sai Yoga.* New Delhi, India: Macmillan, 1983.

Fanibunda, E. B. *The Vision of the Divine.* Bombay, India: Fanibunda, 1976.

Gosnel of Sri Ramakrisha. Translated by Swami Nikhilananda. Hollywood, CA: Vedanta Press.

Happold, F. C. *Mysticism.* New York: Viking Penguin, 1963.

Healers and the Healing Process. Edited by George W. Meek. Wheaton, IL: Theosophical Publishing House, 1977.

Huxley, Aldous. *The Perennial Philosophy.* San Bernadino, CA: Borgo Press, 1990.

Kanu, Victor. *Sai Baba, God Incarnate.* London: Sawbridge, 1981.

Kasturi, N. *The Life of Bhagavan Sri Satya Sai Baba.* Puttaparthi, India: Prasanthi Nilayam Press.

———. *Sathya Sai Speaks,* Volumes 1–11, Discourses from 1953–1982. Sri Sathya Books and Publications, 1962. Prasanthi Nilayam, Anantapur District, A. P., India 515134.

———. *Sathyam, Shivam Sundaram.* Four volume biography. Bangalore, India: Sri Sathya Sai Publications and Education Foundation. Vol. 1, 1960; Vol. 2, 1968; Vol. 3, 1972; Vol. 4, 1980.

Mason, Peggy and Ron Laing. *Sathya Sai Baba: The Embodiment of Love.* Norwich, England: Pilgrim Books, 1987.

Murphet, Howard. *Hammer on the Mountain: Life of Henry Steel Olcott, 1832–1907.* Wheaton, IL: Theosophical, 1972.

———. *Sai Baba, Avatar: A New Journey into Power and Glory.* San Diego, CA: Birth Day, 1977; London: Grafton Books, 1985.

————. *Sai Baba: Man of Miracles*. York Beach, ME: Samuel Weiser, 1992.

————. *When Daylight Comes: Biography of Helena Petrovna Blavatsky*. Wheaton, IL: Quest Books, 1975.

Narada. *Narada's Bhakti Sutras*. Madras, India: Sri Ramakrishna Math Press, 1972.

Nicholson, Reynold A. *The Mystics of Islam*. London: G. Bell & Sons, 1914.

Norelli-Bachelet, Patrizia. *The Hidden Manna*. Accord, NY: Aeon Books, 1976.

The Oxford Dictionary of Quotations. Oxford: Oxford University Press, 1955.

Purnaiya, Nagamani. *The Divine Leelas of Bhagavan Sri Satya Sai Baba*. Bangalore, India: Purnaiya, 1969.

Roberts, Jane. *Seth Speaks*. Englewood Cliffs, NJ: Prentice-Hall, 1972.

Robinson, Dr., and Dr. Ruhela, eds. *Sai Baba and His Message: A Challenge to Behavioral Science*. New Delhi, India: Vikas, 1976.

Sai Baba. *Sathya Sai Speaks*. Puttaparti, India: Sai Publications, 1958.

Sandweiss, Samuel H. *Sai Baba: The Holy Man and the Psychiatrist*. San Diego, CA: Birth Day, 1975.

Shiva Purana. Edited by J. L. Shastri. Delhi: Motilal Banarsidass, 1969.

Sri Aurobindo. *The Hidden Manner*. Pondicherry, India: Sri Aurobindo Press.

Swamiji, H. H. Narasimha. *Life of Sai Baba*. Madras, India: All India Sai Samaj, 1955.

The Tibetan Book of the Dead. Oxford: Oxford University Press, 1960.

Swami Vireswarananda. *Introduction to Brahma-Sutras*. Calcutta, India: Adwaitha Ashrama, 1970.

Howard Murphet was born in Tasmania, Australia in the early part of this century. He attended Hobart Teachers' College and the University of Tasmania. After serving in the British Army during World War II, he worked as a freelance journalist, a profession that allowed him to tour Europe with his wife. Murphet then went to India to study Indian spiritual philosophy where he met Sai Baba and spent six years studying with him while continuing to write about spiritual subjects. When he left India in 1970, he spent a year helping establish the first Sai bookshop in the United States at Tustin, California and then returned to Australia to continue his writing career. He currently lives with his wife in Australia.

Among the books Murphet has authored are *Hammer on the Mountain* (Theosophical Publishing Co.), *Sai Baba: Man of Miracles* (Samuel Weiser), and *Sai Baba, Avatar* (Birth Day).